Intimations

Intimations

The Cinema of Wojciech Has

✦

Annette Insdorf

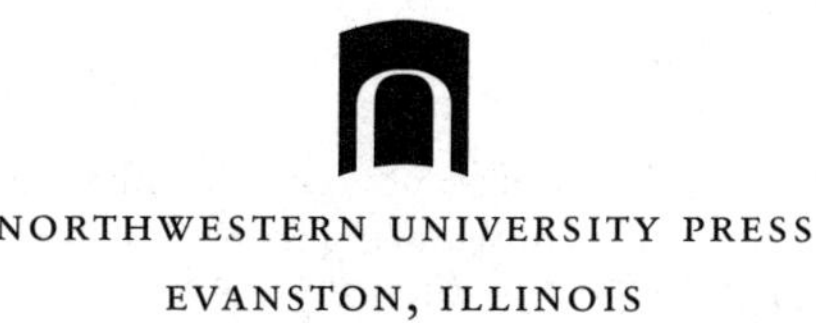

NORTHWESTERN UNIVERSITY PRESS

EVANSTON, ILLINOIS

Northwestern University Press
www.nupress.northwestern.edu

Printed in the United States of America

10 9 8 7 6 5 4 3 2 1

Library of Congress Cataloging-in-Publication Data

Names: Insdorf, Annette, author.
Title: Intimations : the cinema of Wojciech Has / Annette Insdorf.
Description: Evanston, Ill. : Northwestern University Press, 2017. | Includes
    bibliographical references and index.
Identifiers: LCCN 2016050473| ISBN 9780810135055 (cloth : alk. paper) | ISBN
    9780810135048 (pbk. : alk. paper) | ISBN 9780810135062 (e-book)
Subjects: LCSH: Has, Wojciech J. (Wojciech Jerzy), 1925-2000—Criticism and
    interpretation. | Motion picture producers and directors—Poland—Biography. |
    Motion pictures—Poland—History—20th century.
Classification: LCC PN1998.3.H3697 I57 2017 | DDC 791.43023092—dc23
LC record available at https://lccn.loc.gov/2016050473

In memory of Maria Kornatowska
and of Anka Pajewska

CONTENTS

Acknowledgments *ix*

Introduction 3

Chapter 1
The Noose (Pętla, 1957) 7

Chapter 2
Farewells (Pożegnania, 1958) 15

Chapter 3
One Room Tenants (Wspólny pokój, 1960) 21

Chapter 4
Partings (Rozstanie, 1961) 27

Chapter 5
Gold Dreams (Złoto, 1962) 33

Chapter 6
How to Be Loved (Jak być kochaną, 1963) 39

Chapter 7
The Saragossa Manuscript (Rękopis znaleziony w Saragossie, 1965) 47

Chapter 8
Codes (Szyfry, 1966) 57

Chapter 9
The Doll (Lalka, 1968) 65

Chapter 10
The Hourglass Sanatorium (Sanatorium pod klepsydrą, 1973) 71

Chapter 11
An Uneventful Story (Nieciekawa historia, 1983)   83

Chapter 12
Write and Fight (Pismak, 1985)   89

Chapter 13
*Memoirs of a Sinner (Osobisty pamiętnik grzesznika
przez niego samego spisany, 1986)*   97

Chapter 14
*The Fabulous Journey of Balthazar Kober
(Niezwykła podróż Baltazara Kobera, 1988)*   103

Epilogue
Łódź Film School   109

Appendix
Early Shorts   115

Filmography   121

Notes   129

Bibliography   137

Index   141

I am very grateful to Michael Levine, my editor at Northwestern University Press, for shepherding this project and to the Georges Borchardt agency for its patient work on my behalf. The book would not have been possible without the support of the Adam Mickiewicz Institute in Warsaw, especially Paweł Potoroczyn and Grzegorz Skorupski. Hanna Hartowicz was a formidable ally, whether translating Polish texts or providing contacts during my two trips to Poland. At the Łódź Film School, many people shared valuable memories of Wojciech Has with me, particularly Mariusz Grzegorzek and Małgorzata Burzyńska-Keller. And I appreciate the support of Wanda Ziembicka-Has. I benefited from Justin Restivo's assistance in manuscript preparation and from Rob Brink's wise counsel for all things electronic. And, as always, I thank Mark Ethan Toporek for being not only an insightful first reader but the most supportive mate.

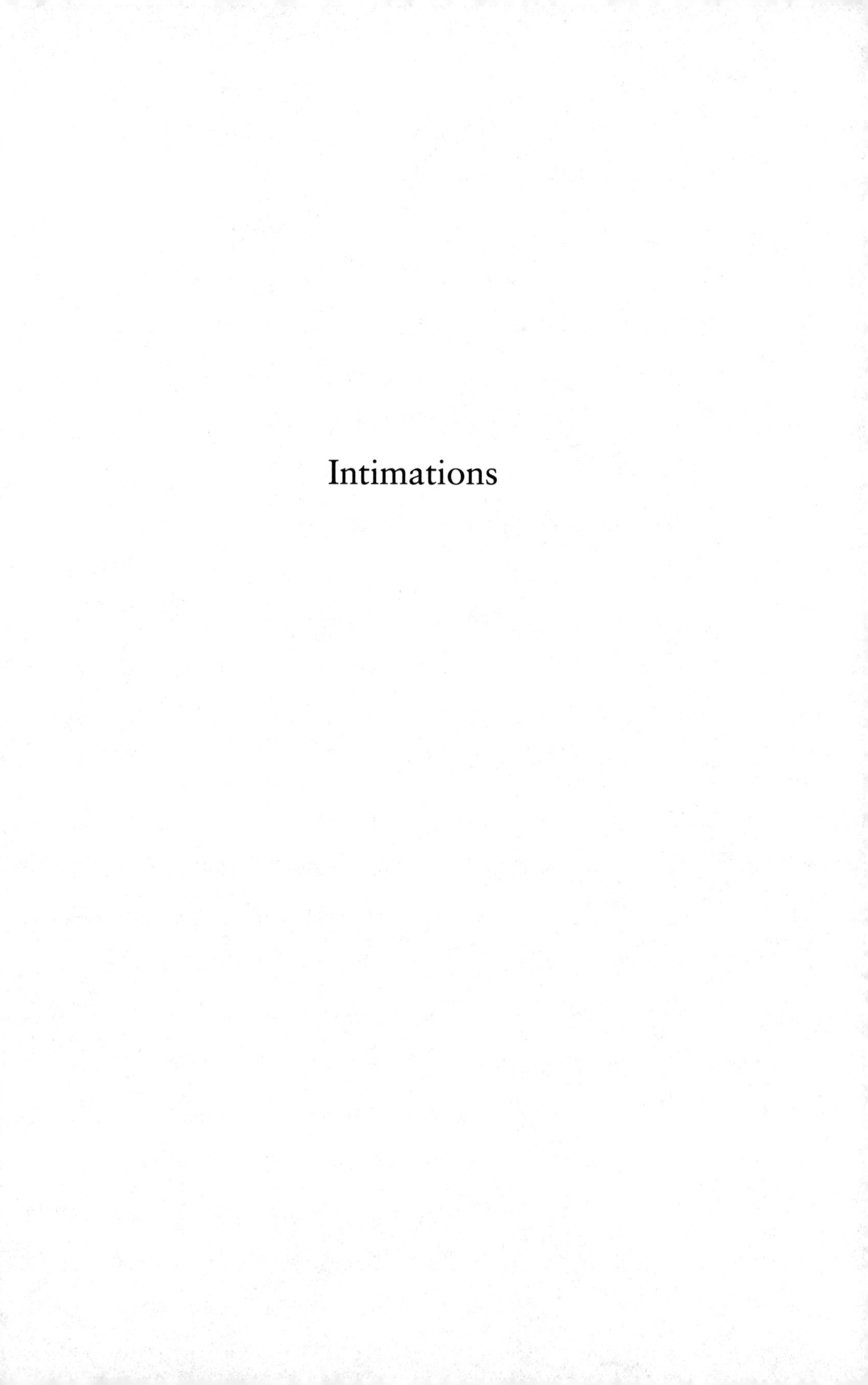

Intimations

With great delight, I have been teaching Polish cinema at Columbia University for many years, focusing on the work of Andrzej Wajda, Roman Polanski, Krzysztof Zanussi, and Krzysztof Kieślowski (whose films are the subject of my previous book, *Double Lives, Second Chances*). Paweł Potoroczyn, director of the Adam Mickiewicz Institute in Warsaw, at one time urged me to devote my critical attention to the movies of Wojciech Jerzy Has. I hesitated, especially because they were not available on DVD in the United States. Moreover, having never met Has, I lacked the personal input that informed my books on François Truffaut, Philip Kaufman, and Kieślowski. But in remembering the impact that a few of Has's films had on me years before, I decided to delve deeper.

I first heard the name Wojciech Has in my early twenties when attending a midnight screening of *The Saragossa Manuscript* at the Elgin Theater in New York City. Although I had never taken LSD, by the time the movie ended at 3:00 A.M., I felt like I had experienced a drug-induced high. There was something delirious about his narration of a story within a story within a story, hallucinatory in the displacement of a Polish film about a Belgian officer set in Spain, and exhilarating in his ironic treatment of men bewitched by seminaked women.

A few years later, I attended a special screening of *The Hourglass Sanatorium* at Hunter College in Manhattan, where my mother was teaching French literature: one of the reasons I rushed to see the film was the name of its director. Once again, Wojciech Has fascinated me, but this time through his evocation of Hasidic life in Poland between the two world wars: I had never seen such a vivid if surreal depiction of Jewish experience onscreen. And in 1997, the Film Society of Lincoln Center presented a retrospective of Has's motion pictures as a sidebar of the New York Film Festival. Richard Peña programmed ten features as a series called "Logic of Dream, Logic of Labyrinth: The Fantastic Journeys of Wojciech Jerzy Has." Although I did not see all the films, *The Noose* was a revelation: it was hard to believe that this stark poetic drama—about a lucid alcoholic who knows he will not succeed in kicking the habit—was a first feature for Has as well as for his lead actor, Gustaw Holoubek, and cinematographer, Mieczysław Jahoda. I was writing my book about Kieślowski's work and realized that his *Blind Chance* had deep connections to *The Noose*. Given that both films poetically convey existential despair through formal choices that include a circular narration, perhaps Has's drama had influenced Kieślowski.

Every year, the Polish film critic and Łódź Film School professor Maria Kornatowska came to the New York Film Festival. During our frequent talks, she encouraged my interest in Has's work, maintaining that he was a true master. Upon reading her incisive monograph ". . . Yet We Do Not Know What Will Become of Us,"[1] I had to agree. In only ten pages, she managed to articulate what was unique and provocative about his cinema and to contextualize it in a pungent remark, calling Poland's Theatre of the Absurd "the most genuine truth about the so-called great constructions of socialism."[2] The final decision to write this book came from my discussions with Hanna Kosińska Hartowicz, a New York–based graduate of the Łódź Film School who knew Has (as well as the more renowned Polish filmmakers whose work entranced me). She offered to help with my research and indeed proved invaluable as a knowledgeable translator, witness, and accomplice. She accompanied me to Warsaw in June of 2014, where—with the assistance of Grzegorz Skorupski—I was able to interview Has's former students from the Łódź Film School as well as his collaborators.

There I learned that Wojciech Has was an intransigent individualist, a chain-smoking nonconformist who spoke little but whose words meant a great deal to his pupils and colleagues. He never joined the Communist Party and often eluded censorship by adapting novels set in the past (and refusing to direct contemporary films). Because he was born in Kraków (April 1, 1925) and lived periodically in the city of my mother's birth throughout his life, I visited the buildings where his presence is marked. A plaque in his honor adorns his former home at 19 Św. Gertrudy Street. The building of his birth is at the intersection of what are now Królewska and Nowowiejska Streets (formerly 18 Stycznia): there, a plaque dedicated to Has is behind a glass window.

Has's films attest to a fondness for windows, indirect narration, and the literary limitations that define visual possibilities. He gravitated toward long takes and deep focus on the one hand and unreliable narrators on the other (especially in *How to Be Loved*). His films do not necessarily fulfill the auteurist scrutiny that valorizes a recognizable stylistic consistency—those of his early period are minimalist and psychologically acute portraits, while much of his later work unfolds on a huge and dazzling scale—but a coherent strain does emerge through a majority of the features. As Michael Brooke has pointed out, "Has constantly returned to the theme of a disoriented individual making a psychological journey through increasingly complex physical and mental landscapes, peppered with exotic props, creatures and automata. . . . Has generally used these settings as a springboard for his own bizarre imagination, realising bewilderingly intricate storylines in a distinctly Wellesian style (deep focus, elaborate camera movements, ornate decor and costumes)."[3] The oneiric quality of his work brings to mind something his former student Małgorzata Burzyńska-Keller told me in July of 2015: Has liked to quote a line from the Talmud, "An uninterpreted dream is like an unopened letter."

His work feels quite distinct from that of other leading Polish filmmakers. If Wajda has been drawn to political, historical, or theatrical visions—foregrounding the possibility of individual nobility—Has seemed leery of these options. In Marek Haltof's words, "Has ignored history and politics, that fateful fascination of Polish cinema, did not take political stands, and trusted his own imagination."[4] If Kieślowski invoked the possibility of love as a salvation in *Three Colors: Blue, White, Red*, Has's characters rarely say "I love you." If Zanussi has often dramatized ethical tensions among individuals in contemporary settings, Has was a prose poet of solitude and alienation. A formalist rather than a realist, he crafted stories that explore yearning, weakness, and loss. In the documentary *Traces* (2012), devoted to his legacy, he says on camera, "During Stalinism, we learned that content was important, not form. I think the opposite." And in the excellent catalogue *Era New Horizons* edited by Robert Kardzis (2010), he is quoted as lamenting a tendency of Polish cinema: "Screens were dominated by reports with psychological sauce."[5] This magnificently illustrated book followed a retrospective in Wrocław that reignited interest in Has's work. As Ewa Mazierska has written, "Has is the 'great unknown' of Polish cinema. . . . His earlier films were only recently released on DVD in Poland and his late works, made in the 1980s, are available in France, but not in his native country. With this is connected another paradox of Has's afterlife and the reason why his retrospective was such a hit in Wrocław: he is regarded as somebody catering for cosmopolitan rather than 'purely' Polish taste and therefore situated on the margin of Polish cinema. The retrospective offered an opportunity to test this opinion."[6]

His films seem quintessentially Polish, beginning with the ravaged postwar landscape of Wrocław in *The Noose*. However, his ghosts—literal and figurative—are universal. One can sense in these movies inspirations as diverse as German Expressionism, American film noir, surrealism, and the French New Wave. In fact, the critic Ado Kyrou declared in 1963, on the basis of two early films, *Farewells* (1958) and *How to Be Loved*

(1963), that Has "was the most surrealist director working today."[7] It is not surprising that Has's movies struck a deep chord with admirers such as Martin Scorsese (who programmed two of his features in a traveling exhibition of Polish cinema in 2014) and Luis Buñuel, whose autobiography lauds *The Saragossa Manuscript*: he saw it "a record-breaking three times" and even helped to arrange a distribution deal for the film in Mexico.[8] Roman Polanski, like other Polish-born directors with acclaimed international careers, acknowledged Has's talent when he was interviewed in the early 1960s.[9] (I spoke with Polanski in July of 2015 in Kraków, at which time he singled out *The Noose* and *The Saragossa Manuscript* as favorites.) Paweł Pawlikowski, who directed the Oscar-winning *Ida*, praised Has during an onstage conversation that I moderated at the 92nd Street Y in New York on January 4, 2015. When asked about the possible inspiration of films like *The Noose* and *How to Be Loved*, he said, "Has is a completely unrecognized genius, probably the most talented Polish director since the war, with his own sensibility and vision."

Nevertheless, he directed only fourteen features and devoted the last fourteen years of his life to being a professor and then dean of the famed Łódź Film School. When I interviewed some of his former students and colleagues in 2014, they recalled Has's singular attention to detail, beginning with an elaborate *scenopis* (detailed, hand-drawn shooting script). Subsequent interviews when I returned to Poland in the summer of 2015 confirmed these aforementioned impressions; as the cinematographer Grzegorz Kędzierski put it, "Has didn't want to be categorized in any way. He was free from all labels, whether religious or national. He defined himself as an artist." Even if he was often out of fashion—as well as political favor—he was an inspirational master of cinematic language. Wojciech Has's career is ripe for rediscovery.

Chapter 1

The Noose

(*Pętla*, 1957)

The Noose is a remarkable first feature, for both its formal mastery and uncompromisingly dark vision of postwar Poland. While the cinematic tale of an alcoholic trying to kick the habit is hardly unique—Louis Malle made *Le feu follet* (*The Fire Within*) in 1963—the existential despair that is palpable in the protagonist's environment makes it specific to Poland in the 1950s. We follow, over a period of twenty-four hours, Kuba (Gustaw Holoubek), a wry and lucid lush who plans to begin treatment to over-come his addiction. However, from the very first shot, the camera narrates Has's adaptation of Marek Hłasko's story with images of circularity that imply no exit.

A large black telephone in the left foreground dominates the frame as we slowly discern a man—out of focus—in the right background.[1] The phone's circular dial and looping wire introduce an implacable enclosure that will be cinematically rhymed by subsequent images. The dialogue is dramatically charged as well—for example, when Kuba tells a barmaid, "If you say 'eight,' I'll kill myself." Pouring the eighth double vodka for him, she does indeed repeat the fatal number. In the background of the first shot, a circular shape (it will turn out to be a hat) and the reflection of bars provide the film's first emblem of imprisonment. As the viewer wonders whether this is a still photograph, the camera finally pans right, revealing that it was merely capturing the immobility of the character. Jakub Kowalski (who is called Kuba throughout the film) comes into focus, holding a gold chain. From his window, he looks down to a large clock in the street that displays the time of 8:00 A.M. Under it, a ladder foreshadows a hanging by noose. When he hears a knock at the door, he hides the chain in a drawer. (We learn only later that he claimed his housekeeper stole the necklace.) It will also be the last object Kuba holds at the film's end.

His stoic girlfriend, Krystyna (Aleksandra Śląska), arrives to tell him they'll "leave this damned city"—reflected in a mirror that creates disorientation—for an unnamed place where he can be treated. She will return to pick him up in the evening and begs him not to go out. This will prove impossible, especially because Kuba cannot bear the phone calls of friends who have heard he is giving up drinking. Pressured by expectation, he does indeed venture into the gray, wet city. In the street, a friend (Igor Przegrodzki) is almost knocked down by a car, then jokes about the name of the pills Kuba will take—Antabus—because it sounds like "autobus." After he jumps onto a crowded bus, a fatal accident ensues. At a café, Kuba has a chance encounter with his former love (Teresa Szmigielówna) and says he wants no memories. Back in the street, two workers call him a drunk and pick a fight, which lands all of them in the police station. Kuba is not the only vodka addict there, as the elderly lush Rybicki (Stanisław Milski) shows up for his usual stay. After the policeman takes away his belt ("it could be used as a noose in a cell," he warns), he sends the pathetic habitué to a cell, anticipating the screams that soon resound there. Turning back to Kuba, he says, "You are free." Our hero is not merely able to leave the prison but also confronted by a more existential statement: it is his choice whether to go home or to get drunk. He elects the latter, entering a bar called Under the Eagle and inviting a forlorn bum, Władek (Tadeusz Fijewski), to drink with him. A former saxophonist, Władek is a poignant representation of Kuba's possible future. He has endured the clinic treatment only to return to the bottle. As he brings bits of food to his nose, smelling the snack before (or rather than) eating it, he seems a lost soul.[2] Kuba is thrown out into the gutter and finally stumbles home to collapse. The next morning, he finds a hidden bottle (which he calls a whore) and drinks before hanging himself at 8:00 A.M.

Through Mieczysław Jahoda's masterful cinematography, Kuba is often seen from a low angle. Whereas this perspective can make a character look heroic (as in John Ford's Westerns), in *The Noose* the ceiling bears down on Kuba's head and ironically makes him look trapped. And when he stands at his desk in the film's first sequence, the spikes from a wire sculpture are angled at him in a way that suggests he could be pierced. At the Under the Eagle bar, the low-angle camera presents Kuba under an ominous stuffed black bird. When he is seen from a high angle, on the other hand—especially in the street—his isolation is graphically conveyed: this lonely entrapment looks most dramatic when he is under wires.

The production design by Roman Wołyniec is not ornamental but narratively integrated. The door of Kuba's apartment is like a window, a reflecting surface that allows him (and us) to see silhouettes. Toward the

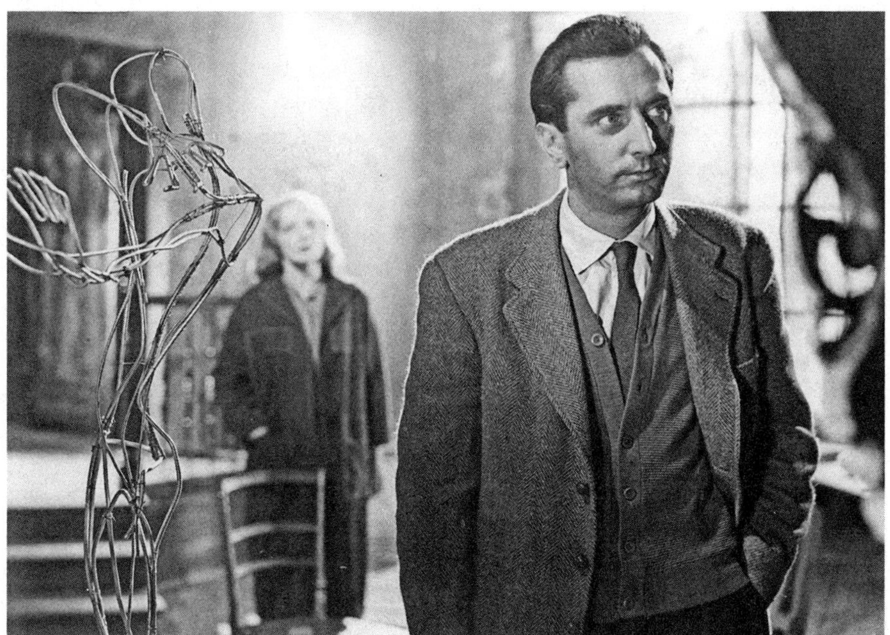

Kuba (Gustaw Holoubek) in his apartment in *The Noose*, by W. J. Has, 1957. Copyright © Film Studio Kadr. Photo: FN. 1-F-402-14.

end, it enables him to glimpse Krystyna handing his sullied trench coat to the tailor—as she had the night before. This reiteration is seen also in his accidentally smashing the glass he had placed on a framed painting; such repetitions suggest the endless cycle of futile fixing. Kuba's apartment doesn't seem like a home: on the craggy, dark walls, frames hang with no pictures; a lamp has newspaper instead of shades; wire sculptures of animals lack substance. (In a classroom discussion, Columbia University student Siena Bergt evocatively likened this to a carcass whose flesh has been torn off.)

Are the empty frames reminders of his desire for no memories? Has he sold the images for liquor money? Is framing his profession? After all, we see him trying to put a fresh pane of glass on a dusty painting that had been covered by cracked glass. The most powerful object is the large, black telephone: if it dominates the frame, the phone will indeed overcome Kuba when his friends call. In fact, the phone proves fatal toward the end in a double sense: he is pouring out the hidden vodka when it rings. He stops to take the call from a friend who expresses disappointment in him and then drinks the rest of the bottle's contents before hanging himself with the phone's cord.

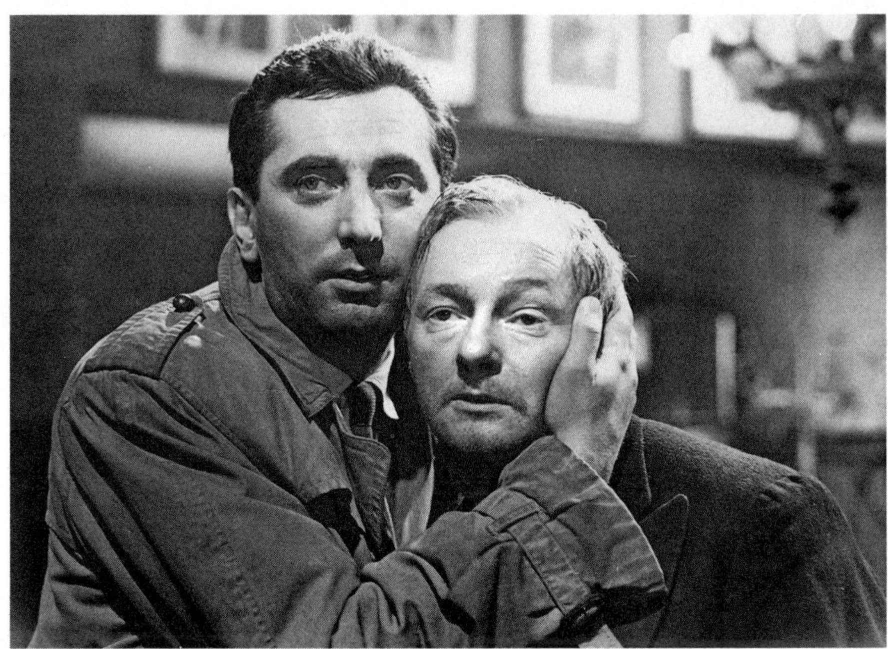

Kuba (Gustaw Holoubek) and Władek (Tadeusz Fijewski) in the bar of *The Noose*, by W. J. Has, 1957. Copyright © Film Studio Kadr. Photo: FN. 1-F-402-103.

The film's resonant circularity is formal as well as philosophical. The noose forms an actual loop, the large clock a figurative one, introducing the film's emphasis on time itself as an ordeal. This circular entrapment is invoked by Władek when he describes the endless cycle of hospital walls.

Since Kuba accidentally meets a former love in a café at the beginning, even the past has encircled him. The number eight provides an enclosed spiral, encircling a film that begins at 8:00 A.M. and ends at 8:00 the next morning. A little girl jumping rope is the film's first active "noose," glimpsed by Kuba from the window of his apartment. He watches her a second time while on the phone with a friend who reminds him that Krystyna often left Kuba because of his drinking but always returned: at this moment, the child skips with her rope out of the frame and then repeatedly skips back in. The shot is recalled when another girl is seen from the café window. An abandoned carousel is in front of the police station. And the gold necklace Kuba holds is a more passive noose. It too rhymes, with a painted advertisement outside his window of a woman wearing a necklace. In an unpublished paper of May 2016, Columbia University student Isabel Robinson perceived that "the symbol of an infinite loop, a number eight turned on its gracefully rounded side, permeates

Wojciech Has's body of work. His films betray an obsession with the duality contained in the icon: the double loop paradoxically suggests both infinitude and enclosure. . . . The tension between endless possibility and hopeless repetition is a crucial problem of existence that Has tackles with his films. Specifically, he frequently engages with the tension between time as a linear entity and time as a cyclical one."

The sound track is expressive as well, from Tadeusz Baird's score in the opening to the loud phone in subsequent scenes or the doorbell in the final scene. The violin that we hear in the background of Kuba's apartment turns out to be diegetic (i.e., music that emanates from or surrounds the characters) as a neighbor practices. Music accompanies the protagonist throughout—for example, when he arrives at the café, where a duo is rehearsing. In the bar, a blind accordionist sings about gloom. And when the former saxophonist faces the camera, describing the endless white walls in the hospital, churning music complements his monologue. Perhaps Władek's ghostly presence is invoked when saxophone music is heard just before Kuba hangs himself.

The vision in *The Noose* is of a Poland void of warmth or meaning. The police sergeant says, "I fought with the Partisans for a better Poland. Where is it? You can all go to hell." As in *Ashes and Diamonds*, a beautiful blonde woman named Krystyna represents possible salvation for the conflicted hero (her very name invoking Christ); but in both cases, he chooses a fatal alternative of tragic waste. If Wajda's last image was a high-angle shot of Maciek's crumpled body on a garbage heap, Has ends his film with the painted advertisement of a woman outside the window. The necklace she wears provides another noose, while her unchanging, omniscient gaze suggests a derisive indifference to human suffering.

Is anyone untainted in this landscape? An open bottle of milk next to the ladder of the film's opening introduces innocence, as does a little girl jumping rope under Kuba's window. He glimpses another child playing with a rope at the café, where a woman rejects the girl before ascending the stairs in a man's embrace. When Kuba asks for directions to the nearest bar, it's the children who all point him to Under the Eagle, probably because their fathers drink there. The loss of innocence is a theme informed by bottles and bars, especially given an early scene of a bottle collector entering the space under Kuba's window. The empties for which he asks are certainly not from milk but vodka and beer. In his book *Polish National Cinema*, Marek Haltof situates *The Noose* in terms of a "black realism," as outlined by Ewelina Nurczyńska-Fidelska: "In the context of Polish politics during the 1950s, every attempt at representing the darker side of everyday life became explicitly a political act. Hooliganism, for instance, was not portrayed exclusively as a social malady; instead, it was presented as an indirect accusation of the communist system."[3]

Whereas American cinematic treatments of alcoholism have been linear and allude to possible cure or rehabilitation—for example, *The Lost Weekend* (1945), *I'll Cry Tomorrow* (1955), and *Days of Wine and Roses* (1962)—the circular structure and imagery of Has's relentless drama leave no doubt that the protagonist is doomed. (During my interview in 2014 with Sławomir Kryński, Has's former student and now head of directing at the Łódź Film School, he recalled meeting Billy Wilder: "He said he loved *Pętla* and that it was better than his *Lost Weekend*.") It is thus closer to *Leaving Las Vegas* (1995). But if Mike Figgis's film provides some background about Nicolas Cage's character, Has withholds a backstory: we know nothing about Kuba's family, profession, or wartime experiences. Roger Ebert wrote perceptively, "'Leaving Las Vegas' is not a love story, although it feels like one, but a story about two desperate people using love as a form of prayer and a last resort against their pain. It is also a sad, trembling portrait of the final stages of alcoholism. Those who found it too extreme were simply lucky enough never to have arrived there themselves. Few films are more despairing and yet, curiously, so hopeful as this one, which argues that even at the very end of the road, at the final extremity, we can find some solace in the offer and acceptance of love."[4]

Figgis's screenplay is based on a novel by John O'Brien, who committed suicide at the age of thirty-four. Marek Hłasko also died in his midthirties after a few suicide attempts. Born in Warsaw in 1934, the revered, edgy writer acknowledged Hemingway as an influence and led a nonconformist life in many countries. When he lived in Paris in the late 1950s, the press labeled him an Eastern European James Dean. The despair of *The Noose* can be found throughout his work. For example, Hłasko wrote, "It was not I who made the Warsaw in which people trembled with fear; it was not I who made the Warsaw in which the greatest treasure of the poor was a bottle of vodka; it was not I who made the Warsaw in which a girl was cheaper than a bottle of vodka—it was that Warsaw that made me. Who and by what right is telling me to keep quiet about it?"[5]

He was often a political target. The anti-Communist edition of *Cmentarze* in the émigré Polish-language Parisian monthly *Kultura* launched a press campaign against him. When his passport renewal was refused, he requested political asylum in West Germany. Then, in 1959, he went to Israel for a brief period; by 1963, he was often in prison because of altercations with the police. Between 1963 and 1965, he spent a total of 242 days in psychiatric clinics. His friend Roman Polanski helped him come to Los Angeles, but he ended up in Germany before his untimely death.

The Noose does not allow for easy judgment. As Hłasko warned in his short story "Umarli są wśród nas" (The Dead Are Among Us), "Those who don't need vodka should not dare to declare any judgments about it. If humanity has of yet attained anything stable in terms of spirit, it is indeed alcohol." The reasons Kuba drinks are not explicit, but they are externalized onto the film's grim streets, where a fatal bus accident is more likely than a kind word. One is reminded of the remark made by the Polish playwright Janusz Głowacki, "Drinking is a bit like sexual life. It's a sphere that the state was not entirely capable of controlling. One would drink and become free, or at least—felt liberated. Vodka was our Polish national pride."

Hłasko's short story is a highly verbal rendering of an alcoholic's tormented psyche, often expressed via Kuba's internal monologue. The film, on the other hand, is a richly textured visual translation. Although Hłasko received a screenplay credit, the general assumption is that Has wrote the script but was paying tribute to his source material in this acknowledgment. One can compare the film's cinematic storytelling to a passage like the following from the story: "Kuba wiped his forehead with his hand and started to speak to himself in his thoughts: 'It's already ten. I have to bear another eight hours. I cannot go now, earlier, because I would have to go without her; I would have to answer all those questions that they are going to ask me, I would have to say everything about myself . . . When I began drinking, why I drink, how much I drink, how much I have to drink to get drunk . . . I won't go alone. It's just eight hours. Then we will go there and I won't need to be afraid of time anymore. They will give me this little powder and that's it. I will not be allowed to do this anymore. Even when I will wake up in the night and won't be able to sleep. When I won't have an appetite. When I will have dreams of an empty patio, filled with pits of calcium. It's so easy to drink then. But I won't be able to. This pill will hold me; I won't need to do anything myself, it will do all of it for me. I will have to comply, or else terrible things will begin to happen to me. Shocks, comas, and I have a weak heart, I could even kick the bucket.' This thought made him especially happy and he repeated: I can even kick the bucket because of this damn heart."[6]

The film does not fall back on the crutch of voice-over; rather, its rich production design, cinematography, and actors' behavior project the tale of a self-aware lush onto an entire city and era. Whereas the default mode for American motion pictures about liquor addicts is often Alcoholics Anonymous, Has anchors *The Noose* in a bleak present tense that offers no escape. It is not surprising that Poland's Communist authorities did not allow the film to be shown abroad. However, when it was finally presented at London's Barbican as part of a Has retrospective in 2009, Nick Roddick claimed in an article in *Sight and Sound*, "In *The Noose*, Has . . . tells the story 'straight'—the chronology, stressed by innumerable clocks, is immaculate—but gradually invests each frame with so much dread that the effect is hallucinatory . . . [it] confirms Has's status as a neglected master."[7] While the story of Kuba is a depressing one on the page as well as onscreen, the robust cinematic storytelling is paradoxically bracing: this first feature shows hope in its ability to capture a dour reality in a fresh way. Kuba may be doomed to repetition, failure of resolve, and self-destruction, but Has's future as a bracing filmmaker seems expansive.

Farewells

(*Pożegnania*, 1958)

Has directed *Farewells* from a script he cowrote with Stanisław Dygat (based on the latter's novel). What might initially seem like a love story is instead a quintessentially Has tale of alienation, inchoate yearning, and loss, set just before and during World War II. Paweł (Tadeusz Janczar), the bored son of a well-to-do bourgeois Warsaw family, meets sassy taxi dancer Lidka (Maria Wachowiak) in a nightclub. They run off together, taking a train to the countryside and spending the night—apparently chastely—at an inn called Quo Vadis (the name of a favorite film of Lidka's). When Paweł's father shows up the next day, demanding that his son return home, she goes off on her own.

The film's second act is set a few years later, toward the end of the war. When Paweł visits a rich aunt living in the villa of their relative—Countess Róża (Irena Starkówna)—he learns that Lidka has married his cousin Mirek (Gustaw Holoubek, who later became the husband of actress Maria Wachowiak). He seems like Paweł's double: both men are aimless, elegant, and dissolute and play the piano impressively. They are drawn to Lidka and little else. Holoubek's face once again conveys a weary lucidity, but without the suicidal despair of his character in the preceding collaboration with Has, *The Noose*. The backdrop of *Farewells* is the disintegration of the upper class, whose remnants speak of leaving Poland before the "Bolsheviks" take over. By film's end, Mirek has escaped to Vienna, while Lidka—who has no desire to move—finally has a consummated night with Paweł in their Quo Vadis room. But the last scene in a gunfire-ridden street (we are not told who is shooting at whom, or why) suggests separation rather than union: true to the title, the close-up on Lidka (eating an apple) removes her from Paweł, who remains in the background. (The alternative American title of the film—*Lydia Ate the Apple*—seems ludicrous as it relates only to the last shot.)

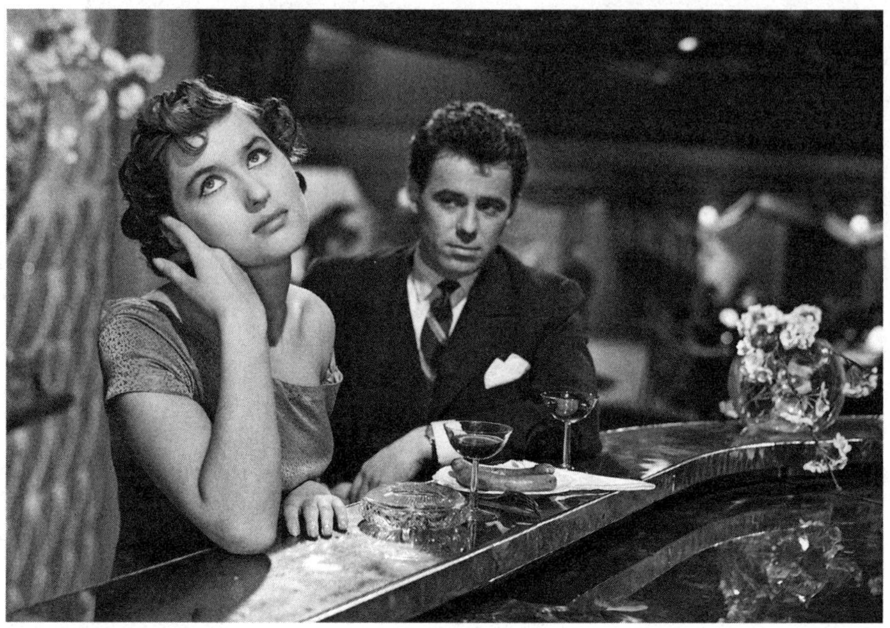

Lidka (Maria Wachowiak) and Paweł (Tadeusz Janczar) meet in *Farewells*, by W. J. Has, 1958. Copyright © Film Studio Kadr. Photo: FN. 1-F-355-3.

As in *The Noose*, Mieczysław Jahoda's stark black-and-white cinematography is integral to the tone of melancholy, and the mise-en-scène often includes windows, clocks, and other details whose graphic energy provides formal coherence. The film opens behind a window splashed by rain, an interior high-angle shot onto the street. After the credits, the focus sharpens to reveal a man and woman kissing under an umbrella; he waves good-bye in the first of numerous partings. A cut to Paweł in his room suggests this was his point of view, especially given the sound bridge of classical piano music (in a minor key). After his father enters to confront him about not paying bills, the older man turns off the music record we have been hearing. (As in *The Noose*, what might have been nondiegetic music turns out to emanate from within the frame. Later, in the Quo Vadis room, the gramophone record gets stuck. In both cases, the interrupted record expresses Paweł's lack of control.) The perspective from an upper window recurs at the beginning of the film's second section, as we see from Paweł's high-angle point of view a street of wartime gunfire. He has not paid rent to his landlady, and, when he leaves, it is from her perspective behind the same window that his departure is presented.

The opening shot is a resonant point of departure for subsequent scenes, establishing patterns of imagery and action. The flowers lightly moving in the rain on screen left are later rhymed in the nightclub where Paweł meets Lidka. A bouquet is on the left of the frame when he sits at the bar, and flowers are again visible as he approaches Lidka: occupying the same space on the left edge, they add to a formal symmetry. Similarly, his lighting her cigarette marks the film's third iteration of providing a light: it follows the scene of two women flirting with him at a park bench and the bartender insisting on providing the match for Paweł's cigarette. At the end of the film, Paweł's last action—before he lights his own smoke—is to provide a match for the cigarette of an armed soldier.

This kind of repetition is extended thematically, given that not only Mirek and Paweł are doubles. There is an ironic juxtaposition of two older women who provide lodging for our hero—an aristocratic aunt (Helena Sokołowska), who has the affectation of speaking French, and the Quo Vadis landlady (Irena Netto), who is ready to sell anything to her temporary tenant. Moreover, the hard-drinking Maryna (Hanna Skarżanka)—one of the beneficiaries of the countess's hospitality—can be seen as an older, embittered image of what awaits Lidka if she remains on her own. Throughout the film, the portrait of Poland is one of cumulative cynicism: a café where the waiter says there is no food but then proceeds to bring Paweł and Lidka a meal (why lie?); the butler Felix leaving the aristocratic family to open his own restaurant, which caters to German officers; former aristocrats acting like adolescents, lamenting that everything is *było* (exists only in the past), one of them saying finally, "Let it all go to hell." The characters seem resigned to joylessness, prewar as well as after. With no allegiance to a cause, the only thing they seem to share is a general distaste for Bolsheviks.

This is radically different from a Polish movie of the same year, *Ashes and Diamonds*. Indeed, it marks the first of numerous times that a Wojciech Has film provides an ironic counterpoint to one directed by Andrzej Wajda. Whereas Janczar played Jacek, the doomed Warsaw Uprising hero in the latter's *Kanał* one year earlier, here, as Paweł, he replies to his aunt that he did not participate in that famous struggle. (Rather, he says he was in Auschwitz, but Has provides no images or details of how or why he was taken to the concentration camp: there is merely an ellipsis from Paweł waving good-bye to Lidka from the train bound for Warsaw to his unshaven face, with a cigarette, as he gets up from a bed.) It is perhaps merely coincidental that Has cast a few key actors who populate *Ashes and Diamonds*, including Stanisław Milski (the drunken editor in Wajda's film) as a former professor now selling trinkets at the train station; Adam

Pawlikowski (Home Army leader Andrzej) as a German officer; Bogumił Kobiela (the two-timing Drewnowski) as Count Tolo, and Józef Pieracki as an aristocrat being displaced in both. Unlike Wajda's foreground, World War II is merely a backdrop for *Farewells*.

Ashes and Diamonds is a stirring elegy to a particularly Polish romantic hero, embodied by Zbigniew Cybulski's Maciek: although he is killed stupidly in an accidental confrontation, he has fulfilled his mission as a member of the Home Army. By contrast, *Farewells* denies meaning or salvation to any character. An existential void permeates the numerous farewells of the film, whether onscreen (Paweł to Lidka) or offscreen (his parents have fled to England and Mirek to Vienna). "Quo Vadis" translates as "where are you going?"[1] When Lidka and Paweł board a train, they don't know where it is headed. Later, he asks Mirek, "Is there anything to rush to these days?" The very rhythm of their movements is laconic (especially when compared with the accelerated pace of Maciek in *Ashes and Diamonds*). Mirek subsequently laments, "Sometimes I want to say farewell to everyone and everything. . . . It's not just the Occupation, but internally . . . what's next? What to return to?" The desolation he suggests cannot be blamed on occupying powers; rather, it stems from a malaise of the bourgeoisie that is perhaps Western European. Even a bartender blowing out the candle after Maryna and Paweł exit a bar extends our focus onto the departure of smoke, or ephemerality: it seems to give graphic form to Mirek's evocative line about escaping "from one's own shadow."

Characters seem to be on their way out, but to no particular destination. The disaffected Paweł says toward the end, "The train has already left. . . . Now we follow where they lead us." They go through the motions—of courtship or work—always using the polite form of address, *pan* (sir) and *pani* (madam). The flirtation of Paweł and Lidka—much like the drinks and sausages they order at the bar—is not immediately consummated. Throughout *Farewells*, people almost eat or drink something they need—and leave before being nourished. (The visceral frustration this creates is eased only in the last scene because Lidka is finally nibbling an apple.) Instead of finding intimacy or fulfillment, they are marking the passage of time. In Mirek's dark room, when he tells Paweł that going to Vienna is his last chance, the clock chimes. We suddenly hear the Chopin waltz that played on Polish radio to mark the hour. Redolent of a time that might have allowed for greater nobility, the diegetic music seems like a derisive counterpoint to Mirek's plan of escape.

Even if Lidka is the character with the greatest chance of transcending her world's meaninglessness, she does not succeed either. Unlike the lovely barmaid Krystyna in *Ashes and Diamonds* who offers Maciek the alternative of love to warfare, Lidka proves self-destructive. In her first scene with Paweł at the nightclub, analyzing those around them, she perceptively sees through the pretensions of both male customers and female dancers: even if she is from a lower-class background, Lidka is sharp and independent. But after marrying Mirek, she has apparently settled into a comfortable cage, with no outlet for her considerable energies. (Maria Wachowiak, who played Lidka, punned that Has's relationship with his actors was "*hassliebe*," hate-love.[2])

Farewells won the FIPRESCI Award at the 1959 Locarno International Film Festival. It also became known for a song composed for the film, "Pamiętasz, była jesień" ("Remember, It Was Autumn," music by Lucjan Kaszycki, lyrics by Andrzej Czekalski and Ryszard Pluciński), performed in an early nightclub scene by Anna Łubieńska (but voiced by Sława Przybylska). Dressed in a striking black dress (leaving one shoulder exposed) and wearing one snaking black glove (her other hand holds a flower), she sings a tale of romantic nostalgia. With long black hair and bangs—reminiscent of famed songstress Juliette Gréco—she is shot from a low angle and dominates the frame. Her song is about a relationship that took place one year ago in the autumn at a hotel; the repetition of "room number 8" invokes *The Noose*.[3] When Paweł and Lidka wait for food at a café, he initially plays the piano melody from the opening credit scene and then switches to a classical version of the song. Later, Mirek plays "Pamiętasz, była jesień" in the villa (while Paweł holds the pendulum of a clock), and, during the following scene in a café, an accordionist plays a variation on the same melody.[4] Weaving throughout *Farewells*, the song sets a tone of lyrical melancholy, which is expressive of the early work of Wojciech Has in general.

Chapter 3

One Room Tenants

(*Wspólny pokój*, 1960)

With *One Room Tenants* (also known as *Roommates*), Has created another formally striking if thematically despairing Polish drama about wasted lives. He cowrote the script—based on the autobiographical novel by Zbigniew Uniłowski—with his *Farewells* collaborator Stanisław Dygat. The characters are mostly young, well-bred Polish wastrels whose creative potential is squandered on booze and superficial flirtation. The premise of unattached individuals sharing a large Warsaw room might suggest the Communist era of the film's making; however, an early scene at a Jewish café situates the action in the past of the 1930s. As in many of Has's works, Yiddish-speaking characters not only add a vibrant tone but also imply a political dimension: made fifteen years after most of Poland's Jews were killed or displaced—a time when anti-Semitism was still apparent—*One Room Tenants* acknowledges that Jewish characters have simply existed as an integral part of Polish life.

Lucjan Salis (Mieczysław Gajda, resembling a young Dirk Bogarde) arrives to share the spacious Warsaw room where his friend Zygmunt (Adam Pawlikowski) resides, along with the latter's brother Mieciek (Ryszard Pietruski)—a Communist activist—and at least four other inhabitants. Most are writers or students who pay rent to Zygmunt's mother (Irena Netto, in a role continuous with her running the Quo Vadis inn of *Farewells*). While former soldier turned law student Bednarczyk (Zdzisław Maklakiewicz) studies assiduously, the others seem like idlers of the Polish intelligentsia, always talking about writing but rarely putting pen to paper. Salis is drawn to fellow tenant Teodozja (Beata Tyszkiewicz), but little develops beyond a kiss (that she initially tries to avoid by placing an apple between their faces).[1] Salis later has a curious flirtation with "Miss Leopard" (Anna Łubieńska, looking more plump and blonde than in her brief appearance as the singer of *Farewells*): they

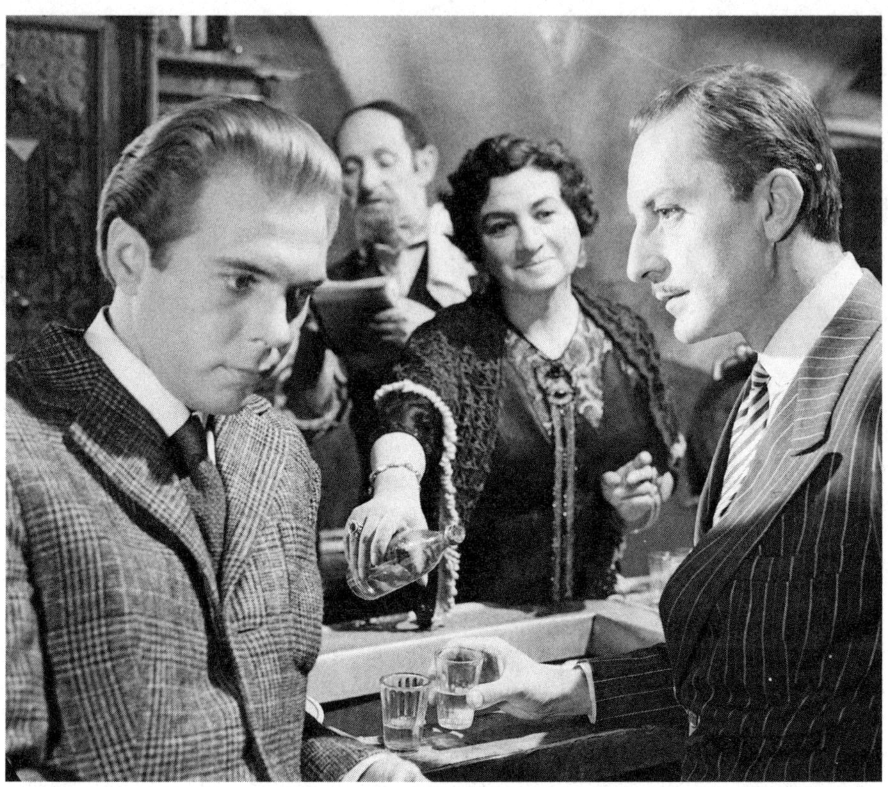

Lucjan Salis (Mieczysław Gajda) and Zygmunt (Adam Pawlikowski) in the Jewish bar of *One Room Tenants*, by W. J. Has, 1959. Copyright © Film Studio Kadr. Photo: FN. 1-F357-30.

meet in a café, where his new friend Dziadzia (Gustaw Holoubek, with a beard that seems patterned on Abraham Lincoln's) is avoiding her. She flirts with Salis, but when he later visits her, she insists on a platonic relationship, from which he angrily flees. Salis subsequently turns out to be tubercular, coughing up blood in a café. In the last scene, he lies in bed, too ill to move. A doctor arrives and tells Teodozja that he will die in a few hours.

The opening of the film is gripping—a wide shot of a teeming Warsaw street where a merchant calls out in Yiddish, "Handele" (for sale) while the male voice-over repeats, "Sark Street," reading from the poem by Konstanty Ildefons Gałczyński: lines like "black as a gramophone record" and an invocation to bring back "my Eurydice" establish the film's self-conscious literary tone. Gentle guitar music accompanies the camera's descent to an abandoned, half-eaten apple. Since Lidka was nibbling the same fruit in the last scene of Has's previous film *Farewells*, the image provides continuity as well as a symbolic touch: in a biblical context, the bitten apple suggests a loss of innocence—an opening to knowledge—that is not completed. Characters do not eat in *One Room Tenants*: they talk about food but merely drink wine or vodka rather than take nourishment. At the Jewish café of the opening, Salis and Zygmunt almost order chopped liver and gefilte fish but end up with only bottles. In a later scene at an elegant nightclub, they are with a comic older couple: the wife demands tripe, but the waiter says they have none.

Has's characters seem ill prepared for hard-earned joy or meaning, falling instead into an easy indolence. "What mediocre lives we lead," Zygmunt laments. Salis recites Latin verse to himself in the foreground of a typical shot, reclining and pensively smoking a cigarette, while Zygmunt picks out a few notes on the guitar in the background. Subsequently, a young medical student insists on telling Salis an erotic story, despite the latter's distaste for it. If Paweł said in *Farewells* that sharing a room with a woman "isn't proper"—displaying an adherence to bourgeois convention—Has's third feature takes the opposite perspective as a given: in this space shared by men and women, there is no privacy. And if all the characters of *Farewells* address one another with the formal *pan*, here Miss Leopard tells Salis to switch to the familiar *ty*—until his anger at her rejection leads them back to *pan*.

The melancholic tone of *One Room Tenants* laces Zbigniew Uniłowski's autobiographical novel, published in 1933. He was born in 1909 and died of meningitis in 1937, having already been diagnosed with tuberculosis (the cause of his mother's death). His father committed suicide. Has's attraction to this writer is not surprising, especially because Uniłowski's other published volume of 1933 was *The Man in the Window*. One of the most prominent motifs in this director's work is indeed the glass pane that permits those inside to glimpse the external world. But Has heightens the internal frame of the window, rendering it an organic narrative component of *One Room Tenants*. When Salis first arrives at the flat, he approaches the glass pane and says, "A ray is able to shine through every window." At the end, Salis lies on his deathbed while Zygmunt looks out the same window at the empty and windy courtyard. When a wet leaf abruptly hits and sticks onto the glass, the visual shock is stunning. Perhaps an emblem of death, it is followed by a black cat suddenly jumping onto the postcard in Salis's hand at the moment our protagonist expires.

If Has includes the window to delineate interior versus exterior space, he uses the clock to create a sharpened awareness of time. Early in the film, standing next to a chiming clock, Zygmunt proclaims, "Time is a fear of every clock." When he leaves Warsaw to take an administrative position in the provinces, the clock stops. But after Salis recalls Zygmunt's verse and says the lines aloud, it chimes again. With evocative sound design, its ticking grows louder just before Salis dies.

The score, as with *Farewells*, is credited to Lucjan Kaszycki and is primarily diegetic. When Salis arrives, he asks Zygmunt about the song we have been hearing—a male neighbor singing opera—and when they drink at the Jewish café, a violinist in the background plays a melody that sounds like "Raisins and Almonds." Mieciek whistles the Communist hymn "L'Internationale," and a female singer (Wiesława Drojecka) later performs a tango-inflected ballad called "Czerwone chmury" (Red Clouds): like "Remember, It Was Autumn" in *Farewells*, the lyrics by Andrzej Czekalski and Ryszard Pluciński grace Kaszycki's melody. Appropriate to the film's tone, she sings of "the task of breaking up," culminating in the question, "Why have our dreams ended?" At Miss Leopard's flat, Salis asks about the waltz we hear on an accordion, which she identifies as the song "On the Bridge."

The music often lightens scenes of visual or thematic darkness. Has's dramas are neither monotonous nor lugubrious; rather, ironic notes heighten the self-awareness of jaded characters, making the action play trenchantly. Whether it's a comic shot of Zygmunt framed by hanging underwear or Dziadzia—in straw hat and holding a long pipe—fabricating tall tales, these characters have bitten just enough of the proverbial apple to shrug at the knowledge that they are part of a fallen world. As Salis puts it, "We're in a gutter, so we try to prove the whole world is one." Maria Kornatowska wrote eloquently about how Has expresses his particular time and place: "Like many artists of the second half of the twentieth century, inheritors of the war, he was contaminated by death. From the war, he brought a sense of the absurd, deepened by French existentialism. His films speak of evanescence, whose base is 'the dramaturgy of death.' "[2] Similarly, Marek Haltof cites a key line of Has's: " 'I reject matters, ideas, themes only significant for the present day. Art film dies in an atmosphere of fascination with the present,' declares Has in a 1981 *Kino* interview."[3]

Ultimately, his mise-en-scène expresses the characters' entrapment. Even if they can go out drinking at the drop of a yawn, their horizons ultimately seem as circumscribed as the street of the opening shot. Within the room they share, the ceiling bears down on their heads in extreme low-angle shots, often with Salis horizontal in the foreground.

After he dies, the last shot breaks the fourth wall, as Dziadzia turns to the camera to utter, "He died and that's all." In an unsentimental manner, the film re-creates a time in which hope yielded to apathy. For example,

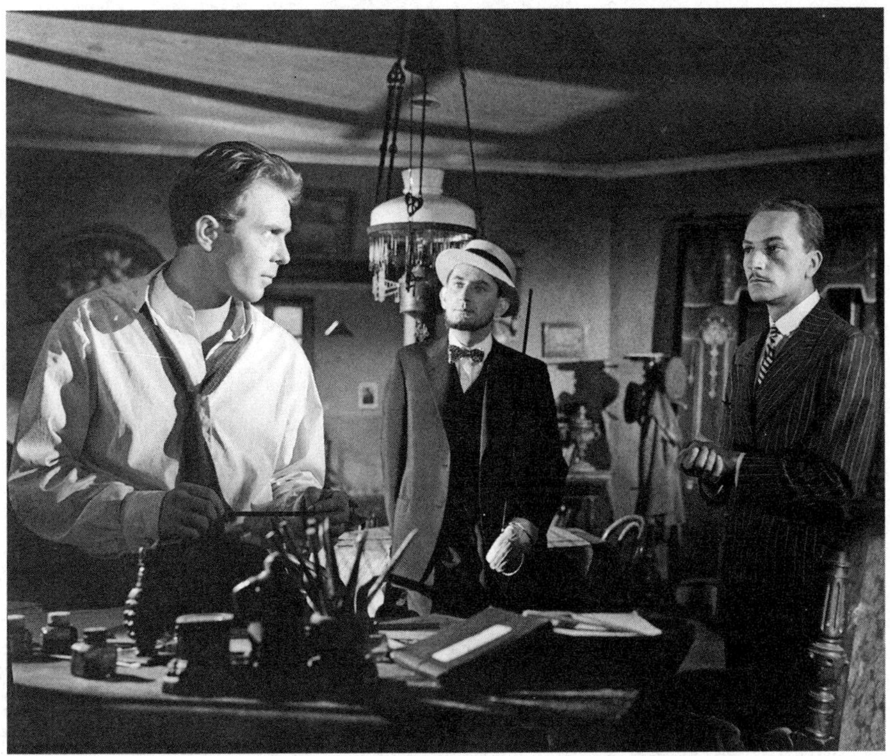

Lucjan Salis (Mieczysław Gajda), Dziadzia (Gustaw Holoubek), and Zygmunt (Adam Pawlikowski) in *One Room Tenants*, by W. J. Has, 1959. Copyright © Film Studio Kadr. Photo: FN. 1-F-357-49.

although Salis is young, he tells Teodozja that it's too late for them to look at each other, because he sees in her eyes what he once wanted to be. Alcohol provides only a temporary respite from what Thoreau—in a very different context—called "lives of quiet desperation." Continuous with Has's previous features, *One Room Tenants* suggests "no exit," to invoke Sartre's term. Whether it's through the circularity of *The Noose* or the rigid horizontality of his third feature, Has graphically presents a world from which death seems to be the only escape. Ewa Mazierska has even proposed that Lucjan's line to Zygmunt, "We have to cling to the sunrays," refers to "a paradox, which touches upon the core of the existentialist world-view: there is nothing concrete and lasting that furnishes our lives with meaning, but we can find a meaning in what is fleeting and immaterial. Every moment in human life is precious."[4] When Bednarczyk fails his law exam, he hangs himself behind a door of the flat, an act reminiscent of *The Noose*. But whereas Kuba hung himself in solitude,

Bednarczyk and Salis exist among numerous roommates. Even if well intentioned, they lack the wisdom and energy to save their buddies who need a wider frame of reference or meaning. Gajda, who played Salis, quoted the director as having said, "His friends drag him to pubs instead of making him see a doctor. Among friends this boy dies."[5]

Chapter 4

Partings

(*Rozstanie*, 1961)

Like Has's previous work, *Partings* is permeated with an acknowledgment of ephemerality and loss. In a post–World War II rural setting, characters seem out of place, literally and figuratively, as a magnificent old villa is about to change from the home of an aristocratic family to a house rented by strangers. Despite the title's curious second half, "A Sentimental Comedy," there is little humor—and certainly no facile emotion—in Jadwiga Żylińska's screenplay or Has's direction. True to its title, the film chronicles a variety of partings, from the death of a rural patriarch that brings his granddaughter home, to her waving good-bye from a departing train at the end. Whereas Has's two previous films unfold over an extended period, *Partings* feels like a short story, compressed and unified in time (a few days) as well as the space of a provincial Polish town. It begins at night, with a train arriving at the station, and ends with another train departing for Warsaw in the dark. The film's protagonist, Magdalena (Lidia Wysocka), is an accomplished, middle-aged actress who reveals little about herself through behavior or dialogue. The film thus prepares for Has's *How to Be Loved* (where the voice-over narration of the heroine will be even more expressive of an actress). But *Partings* opens with a secondary character whose innocence and vitality buoy the narrative: Olek (Władysław Kowalski)—a student returning to his hometown for the end of vacation—is attracted to Magdalena in the train, although she remains aloof.[1] Once in town, they meet for coffee, and she seems more receptive, delaying her appointment with long-suffering suitor Oskar (Gustaw Holoubek). Olek, a gentle stalker, sneaks into her room on the last night she will spend in her childhood home. Their romantic interlude is short and sweet before she returns to Warsaw. It is unlikely that it will have a lasting effect on their lives: as Maria Kornatowska has observed about Has's films, "There is no redemption nor love as salvation. There is only solitude and emptiness."[2]

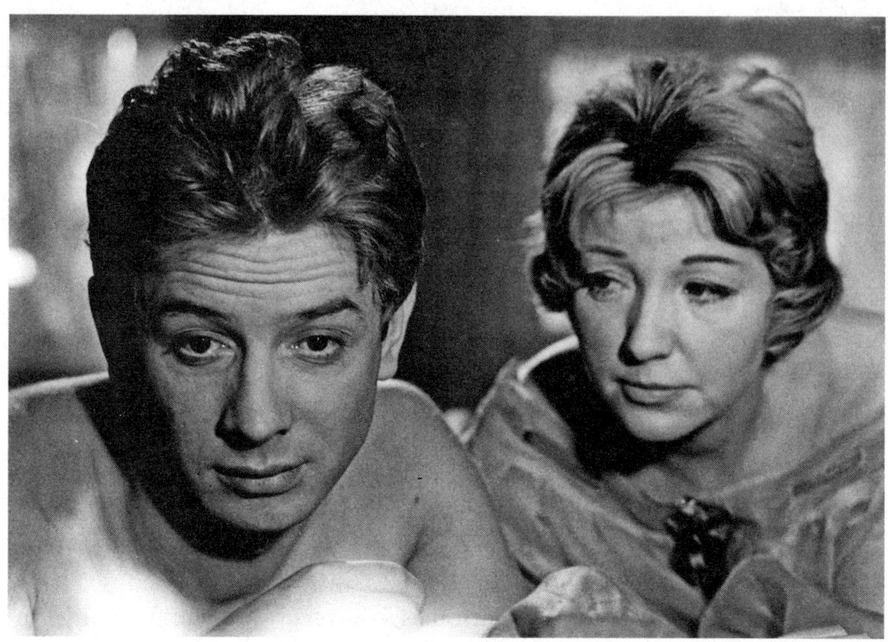

Olek (Władysław Kowalski) and Magdalena (Lidia Wysocka) in *Partings*, by W. J. Has, 1960. Copyright © Film Studio Kadr. Photo: FN. 1-F-1882-1.

The opening introduces visual and aural motifs that Has develops throughout the movie. Visually, the black-and-white cinematography of Stefan Matyjaszkiewicz invokes film noir, as intermittent light flickers on the face of hitchhiker Olek, inside a truck at night. After getting off in the rain, he roams a train yard before we see him in the corridor of the speeding vehicle, lighting a cigarette. When he disembarks with the elegant actress at dawn, the camera follows the feet of Olek and Magdalena into the town, her white high heels a contrast to the rural setting. (Here, her intimate voice-over reveals that coming home after many years is like looking at a children's book, with a feeling of safety.) Toward the end of the film, when she returns to the train station, huge lights intermittently illuminate local dancers performing folk numbers in the town square.

Music is a crucial component of *Partings*, the third of Has's feature collaborations with composer Lucjan Kaszycki. A song performed by Sława Przybylska (in voice-over) accompanies the opening credits: like "Remember, It Was Autumn" in *Farewells* and "Red Clouds" in *One Room Tenants*, the ballad "About the Evening Guest" (Piosenka o wieczornym gościu) sets a tone of romantic loss. In a soft rumba rhythm, the lyrics of Ludwik Jerzy Kern describe a woman who has waited patiently for the return of her man: as he stands hesitant in the doorway, she says it doesn't matter that he did not bring roses; she invites him to enter, shut the door, and sit in his chair while she brings him tea. The surface of the song is light, with an emphasis on domestic details like their cat and dog—the evidence of a shared life—but the subtext is the weight of time on the woman waiting for the man's return.[3] The melody returns in the scene of Magdalena meeting Olek for coffee in an outdoor café: they flirt but finally acknowledge their separate paths. When she then joins Oskar in the nearby restaurant where he has been waiting hours for her, it seems appropriate that the violinist plays the same melody in the background: like the woman of the song, Oskar is in a state of suspended yearning. As Magdalena tells him she must return to Warsaw, the music provides an ironic commentary on his unrequited love: the restaurant's musicians—wearing Cuban-inspired frills on their shirts—perform an incongruous Latin American tune. The music later plays a role in the plot as well: hearing Magdalena's piano is what draws Olek to the house at night. And after he sneaks in unnoticed, his playing Brahms on her piano alerts Magda to his presence. (The music of *Partings* returns in *Out of a Dream, a Dream*, a documentary about Has made for Polish television in 1998. Directed by Adam Kuczyński and written by Maria Kornatowska, it includes clips from Has's films, interviews with collaborators, and shots of the director framed next to a window and later a movie camera. It is touching to see the actors Gustaw Holoubek, Barbara Krafftówna, Jan Nowicki, and Irena Orska—who played Nowicki's mother in *The Hourglass Sanatorium*—silently riding an empty streetcar.)

Even the clocks of *Partings* have their music: the sound track is filled with chimes that mark the passage of time, followed (in the home) by a light tune that sounds like a carousel; time is music, and music is time. In the restaurant where Oskar waits for Magdalena, a cuckoo clock chimes. These visual and aural reminders of evanescence externalize Has's concern with time's passage, which is also expressed by the dialogue: "I thought it would be enough to come back here, and time would stop," Magdalena tells Oskar. After she realizes the fallacy of her assumption, he laments that if she does not marry him, "I'm afraid I'll remain here at my window." As in Has's other films, characters are surrounded by clocks and windows. But the latter is less an internal frame of separation or loneliness in *Partings* than a permeable boundary. When Wiktoria (Irena Netto, once again playing a housekeeper) opens the window of Magda's room, we suddenly hear children playing outside. (The same window provides the frame from which Olek furtively leaves after their night together.)

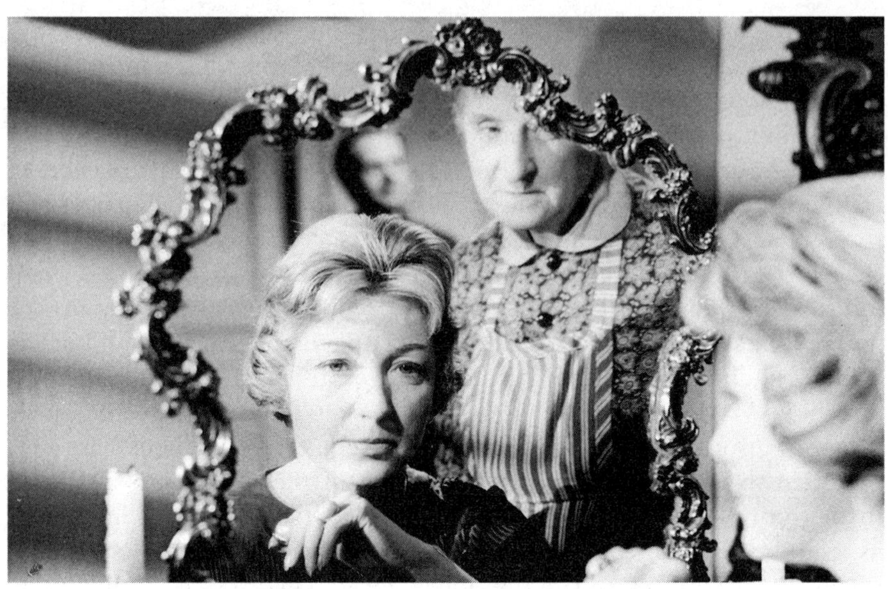

Magdalena (Lidia Wysocka) in a mirror that reflects Wiktoria (Irena Netto) standing, in *Partings*, by W. J. Has, 1960. Copyright © Film Studio Kadr. Photo: FN. 1-F-1882-79.

Opening doors and windows, Wiktoria is the character with the greatest agency in the film. The oldest living member of the household, she is the only one who will continue to reside there through another transition. Unlike the aristocrats for whom she has worked, Wiktoria is not merely a hard worker—among other activities, she feeds Magdalena and the others—but also the only maternal figure. Although Iwona (Danuta Krawczyńka) is her niece rather than daughter, Wiktoria gives her motherly advice and prepares for her future. For example, she warns her not to continue in a relationship with Żbik (Adam Pawlikowski, in yet another role as an upper-class dandy). Since Irena Netto also played the landlady of *Farewells* and *One Room Tenants*, one can feel organic connections to Has's other films of the period.

When Olek marvels at the sumptuous decor of Magda's room (reflecting the impressive production design of Jerzy Skarżyński), he says wistfully, "I've never had my own room." He probably had to share space like the privacy-deprived characters of *One Room Tenants*. His nocturnal mission with Magda is reminiscent of *Farewells*, whose lovers spent only one night of romantic passion in a room. Iwona even sings "Remember, It Was Autumn" from that film, sitting on a bench with Żbik. The house is referred to as "an ark" for the older aristocrats, not unlike the villa of Has's previous film. There, Pawlikowski also played a former count, ill suited to a new era where work is valued. However, *Partings* is ultimately focused on a collective protagonist: it begins with Olek and ends with Magda, but Wiktoria is the one who embodies the continuity of Polish life. With a whisper of Chekhovian sympathy, Has shows how the working class is better equipped for the new world than those who were born into wealth. The house remains, in the words of Bolesław Michałek and Frank Turaj, as "a world of past things, objects covered with dust and cobwebs, things once treasured and now forgotten. It is a storeroom, as it were, of the past winning sidelong glances of nostalgia."[4]

Chapter 5

Gold Dreams

(*Złoto*, 1962)

For the script of *Gold Dreams* in 1961, Has collaborated with Bohdan Czeszko, who wrote the novel and screenplay of Wajda's feature debut, *A Generation*. But if that film of 1955 celebrated acts of resistance and solidarity during the Nazi occupation of Poland, Has portrays a young man who cannot find his place in a postwar landscape. Władysław Kowalski stars as Kazik, on the run from an unspecified incident in Wrocław. At the construction site of an energy plant in Turów (southwestern Poland), he halfheartedly finds work and meets a variety of people who seem resigned to their unfulfilled lives: engineer Piotr (Krzysztof Chamiec) is the most optimistic of them, a compassionate and refined mentor who knows he will die soon of tuberculosis; musician Edzio (Tadeusz Fijewski—in a role continuous with his alcoholic saxophonist in *The Noose*) plays in the local bar while yearning to perform abroad like he did in his glory days; and a variety of vulgar coworkers share a stifling room with Kazik in a hostel. Among them is a former Auschwitz prisoner (non-Jewish) who eats nonstop and boasts of having seen mountains of "Jewish gold" when he worked in the concentration camp storehouse.

The women of *Gold Dreams* are playful despite their drab surroundings. Kazik first meets a flirtatious trio—they call themselves Doris, Mary, and Judy—as fellow hitchhikers: these postwar gals have obviously been imbibing Hollywood movies. Presumably just passing through, they are less substantial than the bartender Zosia (Barbara Krafftówna, in a role anticipating Has's next film, *How to Be Loved*), who is self-assured, pragmatic, and generous. She arranges a room for Kazik upstairs from the restaurant—dark and shabby, but a private space—before spending a night there with him.

Although listed as Kazik in the credits, the protagonist is never addressed by name; instead, others call him "First" because he shows

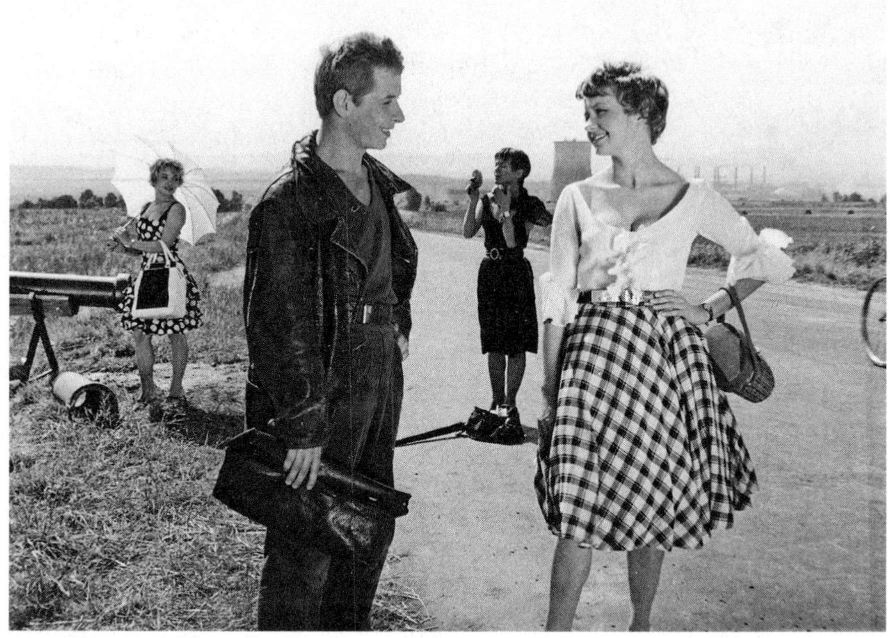

Władysław Kowalski and Elżbieta Czyżewska in *Gold Dreams*, by W. J. Has, 1961. Copyright © Film Studio Kadr. Photo: FN. 1-F-354-55.

up early. This represents his tenuous sense of self, initially anchored in guilt—he believes he accidentally killed a man on the road while driving—and finally in liberation when he learns that he only hit a dog. Kazik receives the news from the man he has been avoiding: "Archangel Gabriel" is how the investigator (Zdzisław Maklakiewicz) identifies himself to Zosia when looking for Kazik. And upon finding him, the visitor likens the pursuit to "grabbing a bar of wet soap." Identity is indeed slippery in a postwar Polish context of rootless lives. Whereas a Hollywood film of the time would have established from the outset that Kazik is on the run and dogged by guilt, Has reveals only toward the end why the hero plans to flee abroad. Withholding this information for over an hour cloaks the film in mystery rather than conventional narrative expectation: as Kazik wanders, we wonder why.

The opening establishes his poor timing and frustration: he hitchhikes at night, but the first truck ignores him; although the second one stops, it takes off before Kazik gets in. Curiously, they are heading in opposite directions, suggesting that our protagonist doesn't care where he goes. Any direction will do, as the film skims both the surfaces of the road and of Kazik. But when he arrives at the construction site, a sense of the earth's depth begins to inform the film. Men are digging below the ground—excavating not only to install machines but also to perhaps find a piece of old gold—and he settles in provisionally if skeptically: when a worker says they are digging holes in the earth, he asks, "for Swiss cheese?" Piotr later proposes, "The earth never lies. But we know too little about it." The location of *Gold Dreams* has narrative weight, enclosing characters who often speak of the border: tantalizingly near but beyond our visual boundary, it is invoked as a space of escape. "Poland is small," says Piotr, acknowledging the lure of exoticism when Kazik mentions the cities he visited as a sailor, like "Buenos Aires, Rio de Janeiro." A laborer says wistfully that over the border one can buy a Jaguar and go to Seville for bullfights. But this lure is ironically deflated when a worker quotes from a French poem, "Où sont les neiges d'antan?" (Where are the snows of yesteryear?), and his younger mate replies, "Dans les pissoirs" (in the urinals).

The intimation of cultures beyond the limited setting of the film is most evocatively presented when a coworker reads a Jack London tale of the Gold Rush. In their crowded room, Kazik urges him to read out loud, savoring the description of men struggling to find gold in North America. But some of his roommates mock the literary tale, especially the boorish lout who yells that only he has seen real accumulations of gold—"drawers full of jewelry and teeth," he boasts—taken from Jews in Auschwitz. Kazik hits him but succeeds only in having pages torn from the London novel. The long take maintains the tension of men forced to share a cramped and malodorous space.

Has's predilection for uninterrupted takes makes it seem like Kazik is eavesdropping or peering, beginning with an early scene at a gas station where he overhears two men talking. His first interchange with Piotr and his buddy (Adam Pawlikowski, once again cast as a condescending character whose typical gaze is of disapproval) consists of their noticing that he is listening to their conversation at a café table. (In the background, one can notice Wojciech Has's cameo as a police officer in a motorcycle helmet!) In Piotr's office, he opens a cigar box before the engineer enters, prompting the latter to wonder if Kazik is a thief. He insists that he is not, and, in a later scene, Piotr shows him the contents of the box—dead butterflies that he has preserved. Kazik exits his room over the restaurant to find that the three "Americanized" young women share the room next door: he watches them bicker before approaching to invite them out for the day. In fact, *Gold Dreams* differs from many of Has's films because its hero does not position himself at a window: Kazik is more ready to engage with those around him than Kuba in *The Noose* or Paweł in *Fare-wells*. Instead, the ones calling or waving from a window are Piotr (who watches him leave for work with his buddy) and later Zosia, addressing him as "First." The window is reserved for those who look out for him, perceptually as well as emotionally.

The black-and-white palette effectively serves the visual texture and flow. Working once again with cinematographer Stefan Matyjaszkiewicz, Has evokes a poetic realism in some of the night shots, along with a grittier tone during the day. Ewa Mazierska compares the film to Antonioni's *Red Desert* (1964), adding, "Symptomatically, another Polish film-maker associated with subverting rather than being obedient to the socialist regime, Jerzy Skolimowski, in the 1960s followed in Has's footsteps, making *Walkover* (1965), set in Plock oil refinery and praising Polish industrialization for offering young drifters a place to live and a chance to fulfill their potential."[1] When light flickers on Kazik's sleeping face at the beginning, connections to *Partings* are palpable (even if there is greater fluidity in the camerawork of *Gold Dreams*). The elasticity of the frame is appropriate to a hero who tests his mobility, both horizontally (hitch-hiking) and vertically (digging into the earth). For example, a fluid pan representing Kazik's perspective of the socialist building site lands on the musician Edzio, incongruous in an elegant jacket and bow tie. (Hearing his trombone in this vast external landscape evokes Fellini's *La Strada* of 1954, where Nino Rota's haunting melody is played by the tightrope artist [Richard Basehart]: in the circus ring, Giulietta Masina's character follows him around with a trombone, and she later plays the tune on a trumpet.) Later, in the restaurant at night, Edzio is in his rightful space; the lucid lush nevertheless refers to his trombone playing as "one big burp."

The sound track differs from Has's earlier films by withholding music during the opening sequence. Kazik hitchhikes in silence, and the sound grows only when he enters the gas station, where a sports broadcast emanates from a radio. The dramatic score begins with the opening credits and recurs occasionally throughout the film. After the credits, the sound track returns to diegetic when Kazik hears a man whistling the popular Polish song "The Last Sunday." Unlike Has's previous three collaborations with Lucjan Kaszycki, it does not contain a song with lyrics; rather, Zosia initially whistles along with the radio and later hums a melody. And when a wealthy patron asks for another cognac, she makes a song in German out of *noch einmal* (one more time). Like Has's images, the music informs a poetic vision.

Gold Dreams is not the only Polish film of the late fifties and early sixties to portray a woman who works in a bar offering the possibility

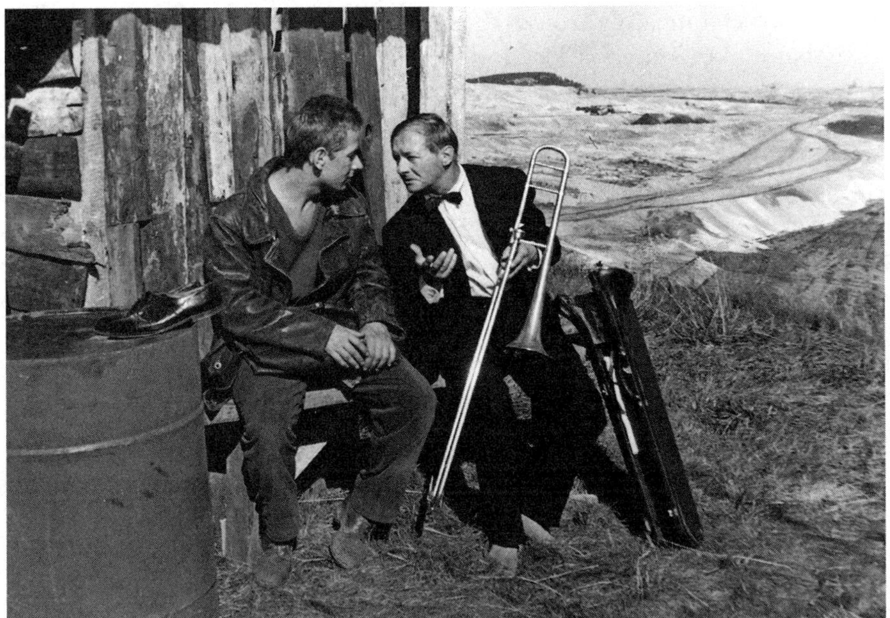

Kazik (Władysław Kowalski) and Edzio (Tadeusz Fijewski) with trombone in *Gold Dreams*, by W. J. Has, 1961. Copyright © Film Studio Kadr. Photo: FN. 1-F-354-1.

of romance to the hero; as in *Ashes and Diamonds* and *Farewells*, Zosia could be an emotional anchor for Kazik; he even tells her, playfully, that they will marry and have a big house (followed by their hearty laughter at the idea). He also flirts with Doris/Dorota (a delightful Elżbieta Czyżewska) when they frolic in the countryside for the day. But Kazik and his counterparts do not embrace amorous commitment, and we leave them wandering aimlessly (via Has) or dead (via Wajda). Krzysztof Teodor Toeplitz wrote, "Sometimes, as for example in *One-Room Tenants*, love manages to be a comforting gesture; or sometimes, as in *Farewells*, it confirms in some way the crystallization of the hero's attitude. But also very often it has a diffusing effect—it becomes burdensome and importunate as in *The Noose* and *Gold Dreams*. The attitude to love and women in Has's films is yet another occasion for irony. These things seem to be marginal rather than central to the hero's life."[2]

Even without proposing love as salvation, a conventional filmmaker might have ended *Gold Dreams* more optimistically, with the hero leaving town and resuming his profession as a truck driver. Instead, Kazik finds Piotr, who waited out in the cold all night to keep his young protégé from going through with his escape plan. After Piotr dies in his arms,

Kazik runs chaotically through the construction site in a wide-angle long take that makes him look lost and increasingly tiny. Despite the openness of the space, the last shot brings us back to the dialogue that accompanied his arrival there: to his question, "What is all this," Kazik was told, "the end of the road." There is still tension between spatial freedom and his lack of direction.

Chapter 6

✦

How to Be Loved

(*Jak być kochaną*, 1963)

How to Be Loved could have been merely a melodramatic tale. But in Wojciech Has's 1963 release—with a screenplay adapted by Kazimierz Brandys from his own novel—an intelligent formalism enriches the story. It is told entirely from the perspective of Felicja (Barbara Krafftówna), a popular radio actress, during a trip from Warsaw to Paris. As in *The Noose*, spatial limitations define narrative possibilities. But instead of the confinement to twenty-four hours that structured Has's first feature, Felicja's two plane flights engender flashbacks as she remembers events during and after World War II. Once again, Has implies fatalism by using a circular structure: despite the linearity of air travel, Felicja's stream of consciousness spirals into the past. Is she a reliable narrator? Not necessarily, given the five glasses of cognac she consumes en route. She is comparable to the female protagonist of *Hiroshima, mon amour* (1959), which is also centered on an actress—comfortable with her sexuality—whose voice-over bridges the present and the wartime past.[1]

Through a series of flashbacks, we learn that Felicja was a provincial stage actress in 1939, playing Ophelia to the Hamlet of Wiktor (Zbigniew Cybulski). After German troops march into Poland, Wiktor's defiantly anti-Nazi actions lead to his persecution. She agrees to hide him, but—during the five years he spends in her apartment—Wiktor is a miserable captive, a performer reduced to having only one spectator. He leaves her at war's end, only to become an alcoholically bad actor. She later rescues him from a bar and brings him back to her flat, intending to protect him again. But an "occupation" of this kind—once again—is too much for Wiktor: after Felicja leaves him in the room for a moment, she returns to find an open window and the sound of a woman's scream downstairs: he has jumped to his death. By the film's end, Felicja's flight has landed in Paris, and no traces of the war's weight are visible on the face

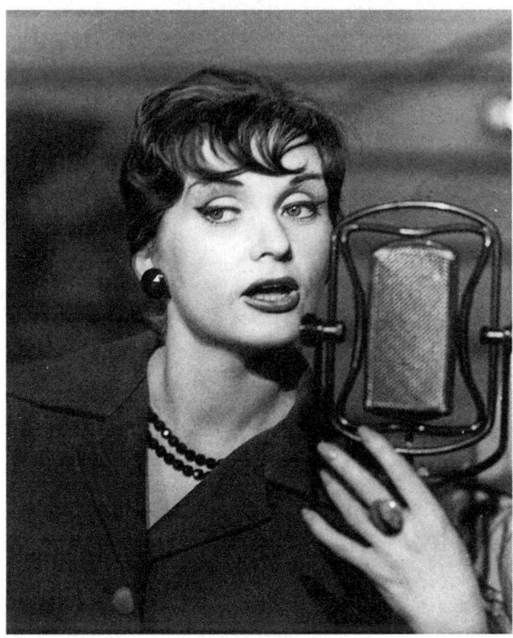

Felicja (Barbara Krafftówna) in *How to Be Loved*, by W. J. Has, 1962. Copyright © Film Studio Kadr. Photo: FN. 1-F-1800-1.

of this successful performer—almost as if her voice-over had recounted a radio play.

The opening shot is a close-up of lipstick being applied in a round compact mirror at a bar (which will be rhymed at the end of the film by Felicja's cosmetic touch-up). Only the mouth is visible, an abstraction that calls attention to the importance of voice, as well as the female self-assessment that often takes place on reflective surfaces. Seeing just a fragment of a face prepares for the gradual unfolding of one woman's memories. Has guards her mystery, suggesting that we will get to know only a bit of her at a time. "I'm the sister of the lonely and the wife of widowers," she says in voice-over. "If I ever write my memoirs, I'll call them 'From Ophelia to Felicja, or How to Be Loved.' The past seems like a bad play now, in which I played the part of a funny tragic heroine, and I have now gone backstage. . . . Better to pretend it all makes sense, and have a nice voice on the radio. I have the feeling I've become part of things that happened in the background. I'd like to move still further back and look at the wreckage from a distance." Felicja's voice-over constitutes one layer of cinematic narration, while the long take introduces another—a device that will prove appropriate for the theme of entrapment. Moreover, Has's narrative strategies include misleading clues that serve to make the viewer attentive to detail. We hear a couple arguing in the background . . . but it turns out to be coming from the radio. Another revelation follows—namely, that the actress in the broadcast is Felicja. After she faces the camera, there is finally a cut: an open window in an apartment is accompanied by a female scream (voice-off). Only toward the film's end will the meaning of this fragment be revealed: it is a brief flashback from Felicja's point of view after Wiktor has jumped from her window to his death. A few minutes later, another flashback to her perspective—of Wiktor's hands in leather gloves—takes us further back in time to their carriage ride toward a hiding place during the war.

The credits unfold over the line of a road from the point of view of a moving car, as we hear dramatic music from Tchaikovsky's *Swan Lake*. Both the image and the sound track constitute yet another foreshadowing of an ineluctable movement toward death.[2] Once Felicja is seated in the airplane, her voice-over provides a running commentary about the man next to her—a handsome, pipe-smoking, radio-toting cosmopolitan bacteriologist whose portable radio plays the same Tchaikovsky music. Her private monologue proposes, "A good beginning to a scenario," referring to the situation in the plane as well as the entire motion picture.

When we first see Felicja speaking Shakespeare's lines in flashback, Wiktor is wearing dark glasses and holding a cup of coffee: we realize afterward that this is merely a rehearsal as an air raid begins. She is also a bar waitress, whose older boss Tomasz (Artur Młodnicki) is sweet on her. From the café window, the high-angle shot reveals Germans marching through the streets. Later, it shows the fatal shooting of the collaborator Peters (possibly by Wiktor, who insulted Peters when he sat with Nazis in the café). Although Felicja is instructed to take Wiktor to a specific hiding place, she makes a detour to her own flat. (We hear the same conversation as in the earlier flashback of the carriage ride, but now we see the faces of Felicja and Wiktor rather than his gloves.) Although she seems to be in love with him, we never witness romantic exchanges between them; instead, he complains of his imprisonment, especially after she says people think he died jumping out of a window following the Nazi raid on the hideout apartment. Unlike similarly themed films such as *Samson* and *The Last Metro*—where an Aryan woman hides a Jewish man from the Nazis—one feels the absence of romance or even bonding between her and Wiktor, the inability to provide solace amid radical humiliation. There is no scene of his saying thank you, or even good-bye.

Does he even know that, in order to protect Wiktor, Felicja submits to rape by a German officer searching her apartment, and then to a younger

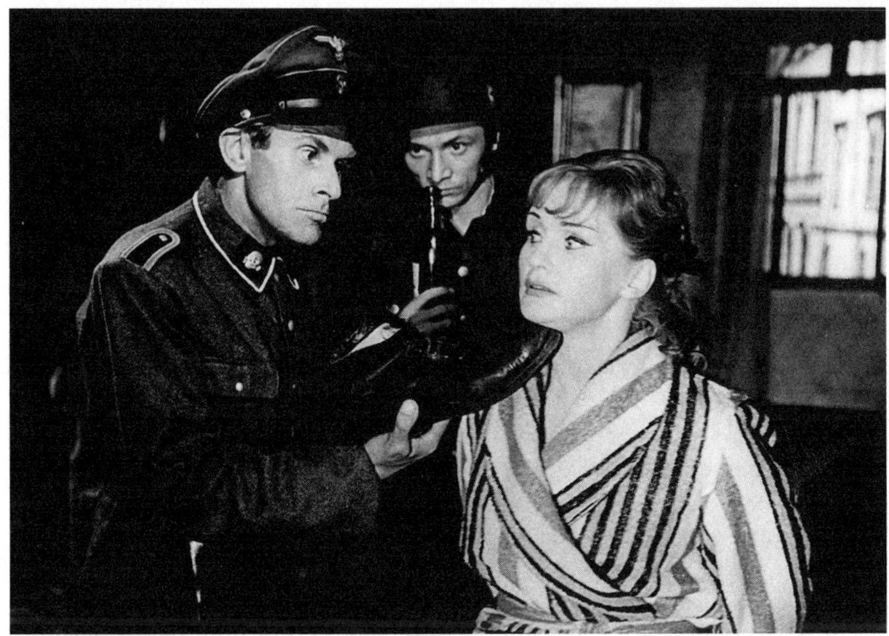

Nazis menace Felicja (Barbara Krafftówna) in *How to Be Loved*, by W. J. Has, 1962. Copyright © Film Studio Kadr. Photo: FN. 1-F-1800-21.

soldier? Because these take place offscreen, and her reactions are muted, the violent acts are dedramatized: a background sound is the only indication of Felicja's emotional state as we hear another woman wailing outside after the Germans leave. Has's directorial choices raise intriguing questions. There is simply an ellipsis between the officer forcing Felicja onto the couch and then getting his pants back up, as if she blocked out the act itself; during the second rape by the younger soldier, the camera remains on the officer gargling in the adjacent kitchen. Since all the past events of the film are presented from Felicja's point of view, why is the camera in the next room? If she heard the officer gargling, did she distance herself, self-protectively projecting from her own body to the officer? Once they leave, she brings Wiktor out of his hiding place, more solicitous of his fear than of the violation of her own body. Her memory of being raped is dispassionate, as if intimated by Wiktor rather than experienced by the actress.

After the first flight of her trip lands, Felicja hears two women in the ladies' room of the airport humorously complaining in German about a sexual pervert they know: contemporary concerns seem far from what she endured during the war. But when the bacteriologist invites her for a cognac, he reveals that his son committed suicide the year before—a touching interlude that feeds into the film's death motif while revealing that she is not the only well-groomed traveler with painful secrets. It is at this point that we learn of Felicja's postwar trial, for performing in a German-run theater. Because she refuses to defend herself, she is banned from acting for five years. But as we return to the film's present, she has clearly moved beyond the political interdiction: the final flight shows her cornered in the plane by a persistent reporter and his shallow female photographer, whose questions Felicja graciously answers. The last extended flashback shows that Tomasz continued to offer her help, especially in the form of the radio show in which they costar as a middle-aged couple. (Her increasing popularity permits her the audacity to improvise and rewrite her lines, to the consternation of producers.) And when he tells her that Wiktor needs her, she finds her former secret boarder and tries to rescue him again. Wiktor whistling the *Swan Lake* music foreshadows his leap from her window. When we see the distraught Felicja beside Wiktor's corpse, the return of Tchaikovsky's melody is evocative: in *Swan Lake*, it is introduced when Prince Siegfried dances with his crossbow, an instrument of death that foretells a tragic end. *Swan Lake* is also a tale of thwarted love and captivity, culminating in the death of the hero. And, like Hamlet—Wiktor's role when we first see him—he is a noble but doomed prince.[3] A difference between Has's film and Tchaikovsky's ballet is that the resilient Felicja is no victim.[4]

Ashes and Diamonds hovers in the background through such elements as casting. Tomasz is played by the same actor who was an aristocratic fop in Wajda's film—and the MC of the final ghostly dance in the bar of the Hotel Monopol—while Zbigniew Cybulski incarnated the iconic nationalist Maciek in the classic drama of 1958. Is Has revisiting the tormented wartime heroism of Maciek with an even darker fatalism? In *How to Be Loved*, Wiktor seems bloated, inept, narcissistic, and his death has even less meaning than Maciek's. (And by 1967 Cybulski would be dead, falling under a train at the age of forty.) Has includes the song "Czerwone maki na Monte Cassino" (The Red Poppies on Monte Cassino), which was written by Feliks Konarski, a veteran of the battle. This hymn to the martyred Polish soldiers sent to fight on Italian soil provides another link: whereas a female singer's performance of the song emotionally unified the listeners on the last day of World War II in Wajda's film, here its rendition by a man in the background of a bar merely dissipates. After Felicja walks past the musicians, she finds Wiktor holding court in the back room. Maciek's tragic death on a garbage heap at the end of *Ashes and Diamonds* seems somehow more noble than the situation of this survivor:

although Wiktor tried to act heroically as an anti-Nazi and anticollaborationist, the fact that he did not die led to lies about his being a spy and Felicja a whore. A line from *Our Class*—the award-winning Polish play of 2010 by Tadeusz Słobodzianek—seems relevant: "A typical Pole—one glorious gesture and then decades of humiliation." Because he walks out on Felicja on the same day of 1945 that Maciek chose political commitment (rather than a quiet postwar existence with a barmaid), one can speculate that Wiktor lives a life closer to Maciek's path not taken: had he survived beyond the end of *Ashes and Diamonds*, might he have become a disillusioned drinker like Wiktor, with no outlet for his wartime heroism? If Wajda's films suggest anger shaped into activism through linear causality, those of Has present anger turned inward to depression, a circular process. The cinema of Wajda can be likened to Albert Camus's engagement ("We act, therefore I am"), while Has is closer to Samuel Beckett's deadpan despair—perhaps "We cannot act, therefore I am not"?[5]

The title therefore seems ironic. In Polish, *Jak być kochaną* refers to the female. And what does this indicate about our heroine? Felicja rejects Tomasz (who seems to truly love her over a long period); she succumbs to rape by two German soldiers (in order to protect Wiktor), and she hides Wiktor but never even shares an onscreen kiss with him. Felicja seems to experience no reciprocal love. Perhaps this relates to the line from a poem by Gérard de Nerval quoted toward the end of the film, "dying of thirst beside a fake stream." The title is less ironic in a professional sense: she has become loved as an actress. Felicja has cast herself in a number of roles—privately and publicly—that she plays expertly.

On the other hand, the subjective, stream-of-consciousness narration presents the past only through her selective (and increasingly inebriated) point of view. Is Felicja remembering only the moments that justify her current romantic solitude? Was Wiktor perhaps more loving toward her than the flashbacks depict? Might she have been crueler to her captive than her recollections portray? One can imagine an alternative version— *How Not to Be Loved?*—from the perspective of Wiktor, perhaps likening himself to a Hamlet hidden by Ophelia. The ambiguity inherent in the stylistic choices informs the film's richness and led to the selection of *How to Be Loved* for the 1963 Cannes Film Festival (although some Polish authorities did not want Has's movie to represent the country abroad). Moreover, at the San Francisco International Film Festival, it won two of the top prizes, Best Actress for Barbara Krafftówna and Best Screenplay for Kazimierz Brandys.

What drew Has to this particular writer? Apart from the obvious talent of Brandys, it is worth noting that—like Has—he was disdainful of

Communist rhetoric and endowed with a keen intelligence. According to the Polish Culture website of the Adam Mickiewicz Institute, "Because of his Jewish origins, he spent the war years on 'Aryan papers' in Warsaw and Krakow. Soon after the war, he settled in Warsaw. When martial law was declared in Poland in 1981, he decided to remain in Paris, where he was staying at the time. He died in 2000 in France."[6] If Has was continually attracted to questioning the fluid borders between history and artifice—as well as between fate and free will—Brandys would have been a fine accomplice: in his words, "For me, there have really been only two subjects from the very beginning. First, when and how reality becomes a tale, and a tale becomes reality. Second, whether or not and to what degree one can create one's own destiny, Providence and History notwithstanding."[7]

Brandys also wrote *Samson*, which Andrzej Wajda directed in 1961: anchored in the similar situation of a persecuted man hidden by a Polish actress during World War II, it is more centrally an exploration of wartime Jewish identity. Here, the title character escapes from the Warsaw Ghetto and takes refuge with the actress Lucyna in the Aryan sector. But when he leaves her apartment and returns to the Ghetto, he is hidden in the cellar of Kazia, who proves to be a more emotionally needy and imprisoning protector. Of the two works, *Samson* is more relevant to the path Brandys would take in subsequent years: "In the 1970s, Brandys's Jewish themes acquired an autobiographical dimension, centering on the identity of a Polish writer of Jewish origin confronted with the experience of the Holocaust. Analyzing the survivor's sense of guilt, Brandys identified himself as a member of the assimilated Polish Jewish intelligentsia reconciling Polish culture with Jewish heritage."[8]

An additional context in which to appreciate *How to Be Loved* is that of Polish culture in the early 1960s. Żaneta Jamrozik proposes in her article "How to Be an Actress (in Poland): The Figure of the Actress in Wojciech Jerzy Has's *How to Be Loved* (1962)" that Witold Gombrowicz's "irony and absurdity provided a language to describe the gap between the happy endings and luxury shown in films or told in popular songs and the living experience of the majority of Poles. The writer attacked both Polish communists and their opponents. Both, according to him, tried too hard to behave 'truly' or 'authentically' and, by doing that, were forgetting 'that man not only is himself but also pretends to be himself.' "[9]

Chapter 7

◆

The Saragossa Manuscript

(Rękopis znaleziony w Saragossie, 1965)

The Saragossa Manuscript has become a cult classic since its 1965 theatrical release. (Although Has's original Polish version ran three hours, in the United States a two-hour cut was distributed.) Jerry Garcia, the lead guitarist of the popular counterculture band the Grateful Dead, called it his favorite movie and helped the Pacific Film Archive in California obtain a complete print of the film in the 1990s.[1] Martin Scorsese and Francis Ford Coppola later financed the digital restoration of the uncut version. "I love THE SARAGOSSA MANUSCRIPT, and am fascinated by it," Coppola wrote to me in an e-mail of October 2014. "It's unique in construction." Similarly, the screenwriter Jean-Claude Carrière recalled via e-mail (in July 2015), "Buñuel liked very much (and so did I) *The Saragossa Manuscript.* I believe that in the sixties, he exchanged the distribution of the Has film in Mexico for one of his films in Poland (*Simon del Desierto*)." The complete version was presented at the New York Film Festival of 1997 and had a limited DVD release in 2002. The image and sound of the 2008 DVD are more polished. When the latter was released, J. Hoberman aptly called it "part *Alice in Wonderland,* part *Arabian Nights*" in the *Village Voice.*[2] The film's original luster was on view in the digital restoration presented as part of Wojciech Has retrospectives in 2015 (including at the Harvard Film Archive and the Brooklyn Academy of Music).

Tadeusz Kwiatkowski's screenplay is adapted from Jan Potocki's picaresque novel (written in French by the cosmopolitan Polish count), set during the Napoleonic Wars. It was first published in 1813, two years before Potocki killed himself at the age of fifty-four. Has translated this blueprint into dizzying concentric cinematic circles, abetted by Mieczysław Jahoda's black-and-white cinematography. The stories within stories are filled with the transformations found in dreams, surrealist art, and Jewish mysticism. Figure-ground relationships no longer hold, as each unfolding tale creates its own "reality," which includes doubling, internal rhymes, and a questioning of perception. The film keeps returning to the same settings—a skull-strewn landscape, an abandoned inn, a nuptial bed—as well as characters. The hapless hero Alfons says midway that he hopes to find the key to this *zagadka* (puzzle), echoing the viewer's desire to weave together the strands of rewind, déjà vu, and circular repetition. More than fifty years later, the movie remains formally inventive and narratively playful, self-consciously juxtaposing stories about control (especially paternal), power, and the subconscious. It certainly demonstrates the director's control: surprising and audacious in form as well as erotic content, Has's mock epic teases audience expectation by spiraling rather than progressing on a horizontal axis.

While plot summary provides merely a schematic rendition of the film's intricate storytelling, a bit might prove useful.[3] Alfons van Worden (Zbigniew Cybulski) wakes up in a barren landscape in 1739 with his two servants. A captain of the Walloon Guard, he insists on reaching Madrid via the shortest route despite the threat of bandits, demons, and hanging corpses. At an inn, he is brought to two Tunisian princesses, Emina and Zibelda, Muslim sisters who claim him as a relative. Emina and Zibelda love each other and wish to both marry him. But after drinking from a skull chalice, he awakens back in the arid landscape, beside a corpse. Taking refuge with a bearded hermit, Alfons then recounts the story of his father, who indulges in duels of honor. It is followed by the tale of Paszeko (Frantisek Pieczka)—a one-eyed "madman" in the priest's care—who turns his lunacy on and off. Alfons is arrested and tortured by the Inquisition but rescued by the Muslim sisters. The Kabbalist Uzeda (Adam Pawlikowski), adorned with a curved ponytail and a long feather wafting from a pilgrim hat, brings Alfons to his house, along with the rational "nonbeliever" Velasquez (Gustaw Holoubek). Thus ends part 1, followed by an intermission.

In the second half of *The Saragossa Manuscript*, storytelling becomes the domain of Don Avadoro (Leon Niemczyk), a beggar who was born a nobleman: his characters lead to new narrative branches that all return to the same tree as the climax of the final tale illuminates the previous ones. The film ends with Alfons returning to the inn, where his now-pregnant sister-lovers reveal that he was being tested: the stories were part of a plan to ensure his worthiness to sire the line. With minor variations, these tales of interchangeable characters are connected visually (especially through decor and composition), aurally, and thematically. The attentive viewer is rewarded—and, upon a second viewing, enlightened—by close analysis.

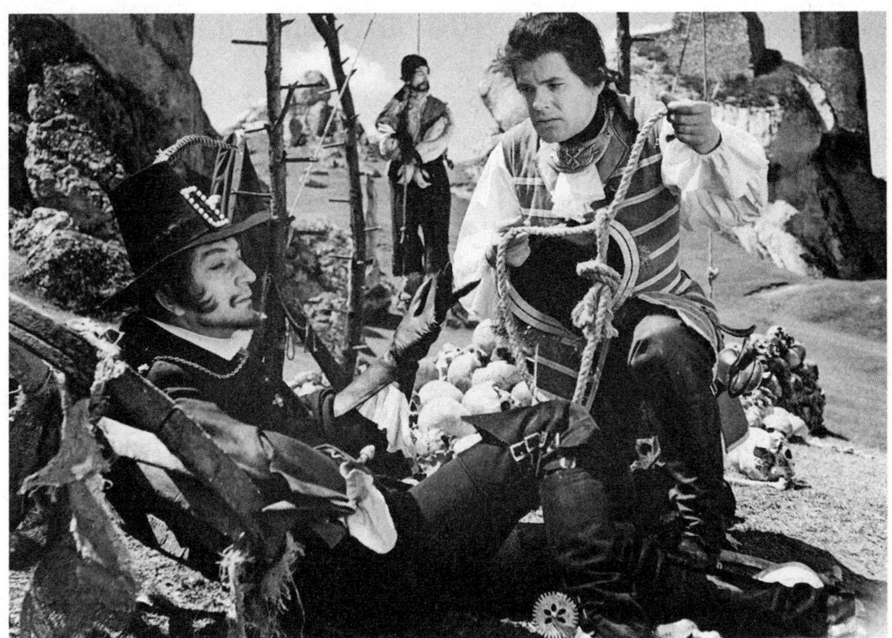

The Kabbalist Uzeda (Adam Pawlikowski) and Alfons (Zbigniew Cybulski) in *The Saragossa Manuscript*, by W. J. Has, 1964. Copyright © Film Studio Kadr. Photo: FN. 1-F-1862-29.

The Saragossa Manuscript begins classically, with traditional music (Beethoven's "Ode to Joy") and a title sequence filled with drawings. But they include surreal images—an eye in extreme close-up, undraped women, a sword in a book, a broken wheel, scissors at lips, skulls—that will recur throughout the film. The first shot is of an officer who walks by a skeletal Christ image. The frame fills with more soldiers, and explosives, in a long take that ends with a cannon firing from the edge of the screen. This energizes the bottom left of the frame, into which a black raven later flies; similarly, when Alfons subsequently tells the story of his father—in which his coach falls and leaves the old man stranded—the wheel turns in the left foreground, a space now marked by violence.

The first scene is really a prologue: taking refuge from battle in an inn, an officer opens a heavy book, where the drawing of two hung men introduces an image that will recur. (On a formal level, its verticality coexists with the drawing of two beautiful women in a horizontal position.) Although a Spanish enemy captain is about to arrest him, he stops to peruse the book too. As they read together, the film cuts to his ancestor Alfons in 1739. (The film does not end at its beginning—with two enemies reading the heavy tome—but on Alfons in this previous time frame.)

Despite the vivid and varied production design of each sequence, we realize that subsequent tales return to the street of the opening sequence, to the same space of the inn (where a table holds either a book or a decanter), and to the identical landscape where Alfons wakes up three times amid skulls. Objects recur as well, from the titular manuscript found at the beginning of parts 1 and 2 to the dangling triangular earrings that adorn the Muslim princesses, Alfons's mother, and Avadoro's daughter. One of the more bewildering visual rhymes is that of hanging hog carcasses, first seen in the background when Alfons's father duels with the gentleman whose carriage overtook his. This ironic counterpoint to the "noble" code enacted by fencing is truly jarring in the final image Alfons has of his "wives": the beautiful Muslim princesses share the frame with the same dead pigs, a surreal juxtaposition whose animal crudity undermines romantic illusion.

Alfons is one of many men who are tempted by seductive women. After his father is pierced and parched, he says, "I would give my soul to the devil for a drop of water." (The subtitles of the 2008 DVD incorrectly leave out mention of the devil.) A cut to a beautiful woman in black providing drink—whom he later marries—suggests that Alfons's mother, Uracca, might be an emissary of the devil. (He wears a relic from her around his neck in the present, and he tells the sisters, "We're in the abyss, close to hell.") On the other hand, she wears the same earrings of dangling triangles that we saw on the Muslim sisters, who told Alfons that his mother was a Gomelez like them. Paszeko, too, has been smitten, with a different pair of sisters at Venta Quemada. (Like Alfons, he proclaims that he is not afraid of ghosts.) We see him tempted by his stepmother, Camilla (Barbara Krafftówna), as well as by her beloved sister Inezilia. Suddenly, Paszeko also awakens on the ground next to corpses—and runs away in hysterics.

In part 2, Uzeda's sister Rebecca (Beata Tyszkiewicz) flirts with Velasquez. If Has's exteriors are marked by male combat and death, interiors are spaces of female temptation. Recurring images (often containing internal rhymes) structure the movement between them. These include two hanged men—the Zoto brothers—who, when they help to rescue Alfons from the Inquisition, say the corpses at the gallows were really shepherds killed to pacify the village (in other words, their doubles). A pair of beautiful women often pops up, whether Alfons's Muslim sisters, Paszeko's Inezilia and Camilla, or the two daughters of Avadoro, who are glimpsed when he arrives at Uzeda's home. The motif of doubling extends

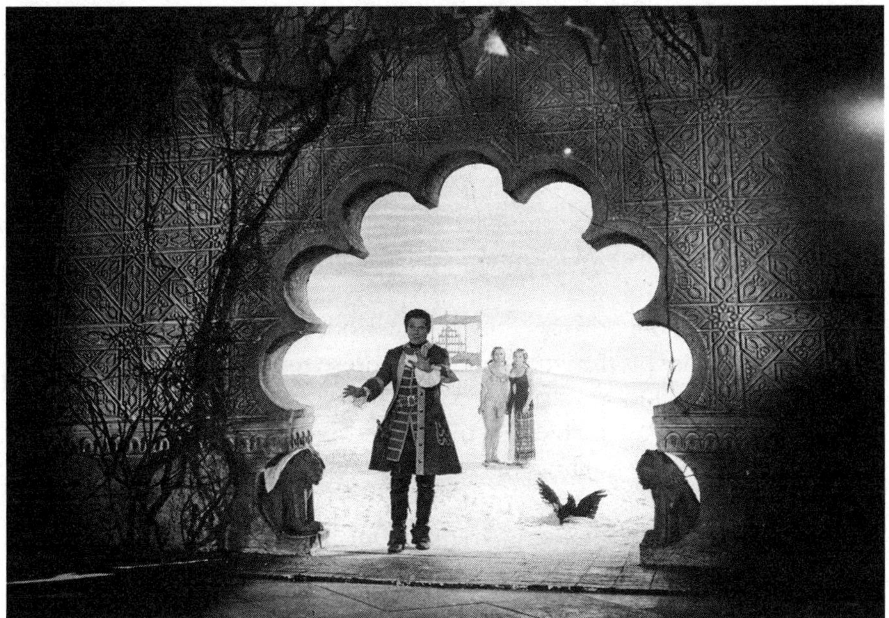

Alfons (Zbigniew Cybulski) leaves the cave of the princesses (*standing in background*) at the end of *The Saragossa Manuscript*, by W. J. Has, 1964. Copyright © Film Studio Kadr. Photo: FN. 1-F-1862-33.

to how both Alfons and Paszeko are seduced by sisters occupying a huge bed in the cave. And when Paszeko's very name is repeated—not only by the priest but also by Camilla in flashback—it is incantatory, which relates to Uzeda's subsequent claim that incantations protect people from demons. The robed men of the Inquisition are elaborations on the theme of displacement, mistaking Velasquez for Alfons. The priest-hermit later turns out to be a sheik.

A female hand placed on the right shoulder of a male character signals the beginning of a new tale—for example, when the smiling servant of the Moorish sisters touches Alfons. (Her own duality is expressed by costuming: she wears a dark robe with white headdress that suggests a nun's vestment or an Arab chador, except for the exposed breast.) Camilla then puts her hand on Paszeko's shoulder in the same decor, leading him down the stairs to the bed where Inezilia awaits him. The hand on shoulder is repeated when Don Lopez finds Busqueros grabbing him. Finally, Alfons sees himself leaving with the sisters, but this is a reflection, and the window is really a mirror. Peter Keough's review in the *Boston Phoenix* of August 7, 2009, concluded, "Recurring themes include paternal tyranny and, of course, the uncertainty of a universe in which you can at any moment wake up next to a gibbet or a half-eaten banquet with a vague sense of transgression. Mostly, though, it's about the sheer exuberance of a good yarn—and the void it distracts us from."[4]

Alfons and Avadoro are "twin" storytellers in the sense that part 1 is about the former while the second half is narrated mainly by the latter. Avadoro emerges as a more competent storyteller than Alfons, controlling the multiple narratives. Accompanied by a guitar, he visibly enjoys the "Russian dolls" containment of his narratives. If Ralph Waldo Emerson proposed, during his "transcendental" period, that around every circle another circle can be drawn, Avadoro represents how within each tale another can be found or recounted. His first is about the flighty noble-man Toledo (Bogumił Kobiela)—the lover of Donna Frasquetta Salero (Elżbieta Czyżewska)—who then tells his own story. Toledo decides to do penance, throwing a rope around his neck (like a scarf) because he believes he heard the voice of a friend from beyond the grave, attesting to the existence of hell. This leads to the tale that young Lopez Soarez—with a broken arm and leg—tells to Avadoro. It engenders, in turn, the story of his father (Stanisław Igar), who forbade him from dealing with anyone related to the banker Moro (because the latter ironically refused to accept his share of an inherited investment). But his son falls in love with Inez (Jadwiga Krawczyk), daughter of Moro. Lopez is irritated by the moocher Busqueros, who always arrives at mealtime and poaches his food. Of course Busqueros tells his own tale, which is focused on the buxom, promiscuous Frasquetta: seated in bed, she recounts how she engineered a ruse so that her aged husband would go on a pilgrimage. On a dark and stormy night, Busqueros takes Lopez to Inez's window: he falls, and it is his voice that answers Toledo's question of a previous tale about whether hell exists: he says he is in "purgatory." When Ava-doro returns to tell Toledo of the mix-up, he ends his penance. Busqueros recounts to Toledo the happy end for Lopez Soarez and Inez, with the two fathers forgiving each other. In a narrative return, Avadoro's story ends with Alfons's father dueling.

The last sections return to Alfons, who arrives—exhausted and deeply confused—at the now-populated inn. He hears that two sisters staying there have invited him to dinner, and—in another "rewind"—the smiling, dark-skinned woman again takes him down to the cave. Once the sisters reveal the plot machinations, Alfons watches himself leaving with them, walking on sand. But as his double returns to the inn, he sees his image in a mirror. As Isabel Robinson has suggested in an unpublished essay, "The presence of a double of Alfons with the Princesses adds to the intrigue, suggesting a warping or overlapping of the spatial fabric that allows the same figure to occur twofold in the same moment in time. An alternative reading is that time here is the wrinkled fabric whose overlap allows a past and a future Alfons to exist in the same space. At first the mirror appears to shatter such interpretations by logically attributing the doubling to a reflection. However, it quickly becomes clear that the glass is less a mirror than a portal." Back at the beginning, Alfons awakens with his two servants, holding the book. Was this all a dream, a variation on "Alfons through the looking glass"? The sisters are outside the inn, one looking into a mirror against the sky. Alfons throws away the book—perhaps symbolizing the process of adaptation?—before mounting his horse and riding off. The film begins and ends in this arid exterior space, devoid of comfort or nourishment, marked by skulls, gallows, and crows. The gaping void of post–World War II existentialism inheres in Has's surreally craggy landscape.

The film's self-consciousness is heightened by the sound track. It was the first movie score for the renowned avant-garde composer Krzysztof Penderecki, whose music would later be heard in William Friedkin's *Exorcist*, Stanley Kubrick's *Shining*, and Scorsese's *Shutter Island*. The electronic score includes the kind of *pong* sound—for example, when Uracca appears—that Jacques Rivette would use in *La religieuse* a few years later. Accompanying the entrance of the princesses' servant, it invokes footsteps reverberating like amplified drops of water, appropriate to the oft-articulated need for liquid, whether visual (Alfons accidentally drops a bucket down the well) or verbal (his father crying for water). And when the Inquisition soldiers fight the Muslims, the intriguing sound design includes syncopated flamenco, which undermines chivalric battle and informs Has's destabilizing cinematic vision. Alfons says at the beginning that nothing will change his plans, but the film traces the questioning of his certitude (not to mention our own as spectators). As Velasquez puts it, "The human mind is ready to accept anything if it is used knowingly."

Darragh O'Donoghue has pointed out that "Has's ending . . . undermines the authority of a book dedicated to undermining authority (and author-ity)."[5] This has a political meaning as well for Poland in the mid-1960s: take nothing at face value, beware of the legacy of dubious fathers, ask who is telling the story you are hearing, and question the illusory nature of authority. Polish audiences could appreciate that Alfons is the victim of mystification and conspiracy, as everything has been staged. According to Izabela Kalinowska, "Has's film comments on the time of its making by engaging in a subversion of simplified notions of identity proffered by the official discourses of communist Poland."[6]

Her article, "From Orientalism to Surrealism: Wojciech Jerzy Has Interprets Jan Potocki," concludes with an acknowledgment of Has's own clever use of the Orientalist idiom: "Instead of responding to a demand to adhere to principles of socialist realism that glorified mundane sameness, Has expressed in *Saragossa* a profound distrust of a dominant ideology that relied on oversimplified, ideologized identities."[7] It is not surprising that Has—whose films reveal a cosmopolitan sensibility—was drawn to Potocki. A Polish aristocrat educated in Switzerland, he was a polyglot adventurer who traveled through the Balkans, the Mediterranean, and China. He became an ethnographer, publisher (providing the first free press in Warsaw), and political activist. His novel was a groundbreaking compendium of the gothic, satiric, supernatural, and erotic. As Salman Rushdie's review in *The Guardian* put it, "Constructed like a Chinese box of tales . . . it reads like the most brilliant modern novel." Written between 1805 and 1814—boasting thirty-six tales told over sixty-six days—the 630-page book is more "grounded" than Has's cinematic translation: it has a table of contents to which a reader can refer for clarification, not to mention a first-person narrator. The opening line establishes the novel's subjectivity: "As an officer in the French army, I found myself at the siege of Saragossa."[8] As each story spirals into another, the voice of Alphonse carries the reader forward. In the film, however, Potocki's "I" is replaced by Has's camera eye, a narrator that withholds as much as it reveals. Phillip Lopate's incisive review in *Film Comment* called *The Saragossa Manuscript* "a surprisingly faithful, if selective, adaptation of Jan Potocki's wonderful picaresque-macabre novel [that] manages to convey the book's rich collision between two cultures, the supernatural and 18th century Rationalism. Has is also faithful in reproducing Potocki's wry, self-mocking, sexy storytelling tales within tales, dreams of paradise looping always back to futility. The problem with such narrative coitus interruptus is that after awhile we resent having to leave so many characters and stories just as we were becoming engrossed."[9]

The sheik says to Alfons, "Everything you've been through was planned." In the novel, the sisters are more clearly manipulators who have orchestrated his journey: by the epilogue, Alphonse can state, "With my fortune, my honours also grew. I became a general at the age of thirty-six,"[10] and then takes joy in the "paternal instinct" that he feels seeing his offspring. Alphonse ends up content, rich, and enlightened. In the film's circular loop, on the other hand, he awakens once again by the gallows, locked into a storytelling mechanism that appears to be fueled by internal combustion. Because the film makes certitude only temporary for Alfons, Has acknowledges his own manipulations. As Velasquez later says, "Controlling suspense is a sign of mastery." Since he is played by Has regular Gustaw Holoubek, he seems to be the director's mouthpiece, especially when he later says he creates the number eight (crucial to *The Noose*, in which he starred) and then cuts it: "I can write infinity, but not understand it." It is apt that an hourglass is visible in this decor, sand contained in the shape of an 8. The crux of the film seems to be, as a character puts it, "One story gives birth to another . . . to infinity." When Alfons laments, "I've lost the feeling of where reality ends and fantasy begins," Rebecca replies, "You mean poetry." Velasquez adds, "Poetry turns out to be closer to life than you think." This elevation of the imagination calls to mind a comment made by Has's former student Mariusz Grzegorzek, now dean of the Łódź Film School: during an interview on June 26, 2014, he proposed that all of Has's films are exorcisms of his own suffering: "The serpentine narration was the form of a child who is cold and pulls a string around him like a cocoon to both warm and protect himself."

Velasquez, who seems to be the only character that is not part of the group testing Alfons, articulates keys to the film: "We are like blind men lost in the streets of a big city. The streets lead to a goal, but we often return to the same places to get to where we want to be. I can see a few little streets here, which, as it is now, are going nowhere. New combinations have to be arranged; then the whole will be clear, because one man cannot invent something that another cannot solve." The accumulation of skulls under the gallows implies that many men have been hung, a graphic embodiment of the fatal cruelty people inflict on one another. This seems related to the hubris that Alfons's father expresses about having fought 130 duels. While he may think of himself as honorable, we see how ignoble he is when he decides to leave for his castle in the Ardennes just before the wedding feast celebrating his union with Uracca: he doesn't even pay the man who has prepared the food.

Kalinowska has ascribed to the film a "nostalgic longing for that which had been forever lost [which] encapsulates the experience of the post-war period in Poland as it narrates a sense of irreparable personal and communal losses. Such nostalgia is symptomatic of a cultural and identity crisis both similar to the one that gave rise to the surrealist movement in France in the aftermath of World War I, and yet more tangible given the scale of wartime ravages effected by World War II in Poland."[11] However, the tone of *The Saragossa Manuscript* is radically different from the romantic nationalism found in *Ashes and Diamonds*. One is tempted to compare the two—as O'Donoghue does—given Has's casting of the three actors who played Home Army nationalists in Wajda's film. In addition to Cybulski, Adam Pawlikowski incarnates the Kabbalist, while Bogumił

Kobiela plays Toledo. At Uzeda's home, Cybulski stands next to a decorative urn whose shape recalls the upside-down Christ from the church of *Ashes and Diamonds*.

Finally, *The Saragossa Manuscript* prepares for the Jewish imagery that Has would develop in *The Hourglass Sanatorium* a few years later. It follows Alfons's encounters with a spectrum of faiths, from Muslim sisters, to a Catholic priest, to a Kabbalist who is allied with both a heretic (Velasquez is identified as a nonbeliever of Christianity) and a Gypsy. Uzeda mentions Hebrew letters, as well as the name of the Hebraic divinity that created the world with a word. He lends Alfons a robe covered in mystical symbols, coherent with the Kabbalist images on the walls (which include two hands inscribed with Hebrew letters). On the one hand, Kalinowska writes that Potocki—who traveled extensively throughout Europe and especially Spain—"must have taken notice of the cultural traces of both the earlier Moorish and Jewish presence in Southern Spain."[12] On the other hand, Has goes further than Potocki in foregrounding Jewish iconography.

The film playfully interrogates sources of belief, whether religious—characters represent the Inquisition, the Kabbalah, and the Muslim faith—or rationalist: Velasquez is the skeptical outsider to the "conspiracy" testing Alfons. He wisely says to Alfons at the beginning of part 2, "Someone wants you to go through weird adventures," an address to the audience of the film as well. Its Chinese box structure also invites viewers to question movie expectations: must a story have a clear beginning, middle, and end on a linear trajectory? Or is Has's narrative spiraling closer to the "gyres" of W. B. Yeats's vision, as in his poem "The Second Coming"? The overlapping and often simultaneous activity of the stories suggests a labyrinth, or the fluid movement of the figure 8—which Velasquez, the voice of reason, invokes in suggesting infinity. Just as the number eight structured the circular tale of *The Noose*, it provides a frame to comprehend *The Saragossa Manuscript*. If Velasquez cites geometry as a way to get closer to God, why not invoke mathematics as a means to understand the film? The shape of *The Saragossa Manuscript* does indeed seem "parabolic," less a closed circle than a U-shaped curve that begins in one place, rises via multiple tales, and descends to the same area. The very name "Sa-ra-GOS-sa" introduces internal rhyme, ascent, and return: ending where it began, the word is musical and—like the film—incantatory.[13]

Chapter 8

◆

Codes

(*Szyfry*, 1966)

Like many great directors, Wojciech Has encrypted his films with suggestive images, words, and sounds for the attentive viewer to decipher.
Rather than being gratuitously ambiguous, the symbols are part of the
narrative fabric of his tales—and quite literally in *Codes*. This postwar
drama, whose screenplay was adapted by Andrzej Kijowski from his own
story, invites us to "read" the cinematic language that expresses characters haunted by World War II. Ciphers of a guilt-laden past coexist with
codes of honor. In the film's present tense of the mid-1960s, the elderly
and elegant Tadeusz (Jan Kreczmar) returns to Kraków after twenty years
of living in London. His goal is to find out how and why his youngest
son, Jędrek (pronounced "Yendrek"), disappeared during the German
occupation. If he was killed, was it by Nazis or Poles? Might he still
be alive? Visiting his weary and embittered elder son Maciek (Zbigniew
Cybulski), who lives with his ailing mother, Zofia (Irena Eichlerówna),
Tadeusz finds initial clues from drawings made by Jędrek two decades
earlier: many are of boys in German uniforms, suggesting an unhealthy
fascination with war.

As Tadeusz questions people who came into contact with Jędrek, their
testimony engenders his apparent daydreams of a boy carrying a lit candle
across a war-torn landscape. He imagines Jędrek walking through battle-
fields on which Tadeusz fought. The puzzle yields a pattern after Jadwiga
(Barbara Krafftówna) reveals to him that Zofia's lover (and cousin),
Marian—a member of the Polish resistance—subsequently became Jadwiga's romantic partner and was shot after Jędrek accosted him loudly
in the street. Because Jędrek menaced resisters with denunciation to the
Gestapo, it was the Polish underground that apparently killed the boy.
Betrayal is an underlying theme throughout *Codes*, whether personal-
romantic or political. Rather than offer answers, the film poses a number

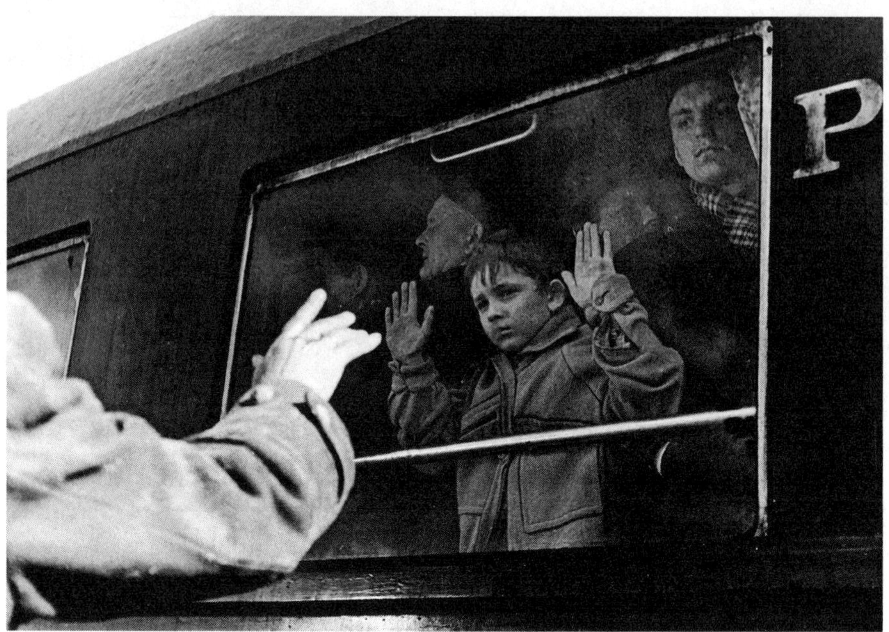

The stalled train of *Codes*, by W. J. Has, 1966. Copyright © Film Studio Kadr. Photo: FN. 1-F-2648-72.

of related questions. Why did Tadeusz not return to Poland after the war? Why and when did he initially leave? How did he react when his wife took up with resister Marian in his absence? What was his profession? (We learn merely that he traveled a great deal.) Do Zofia and Maciek resent him for living abroad?

Why does Tadeusz look at a book of concentration camp photos in the train that brings him to present-day Kraków? Given the Jewish iconography present in Has's other films, it is not surprising that the Holocaust is invoked visually as well as verbally in *Codes*. When Tadeusz visits his older female Polish cousin in Paris and talks about the Kraków family he left behind, we suddenly see him running in uniform on a battlefield. He comes upon a stalled train, whose passengers seem immobilized like mannequins against the windows. The only exception is a little boy in motion—with raised hands—behind the last glass pane. The train—an emblem of stasis and, thus, death—lurches forward. This image remains with the viewer when Tadeusz rides the train to Kraków, perusing the book filled with iconic images of Auschwitz and the Warsaw Ghetto, including a boy with raised hands. Is he superimposing the vulnerable Jewish child onto the memory of Jędrek?

His sudden voice-over provides a sound bridge back to the Paris scene as he quotes Maciek's letter: "Only now do I have the certitude that Jędrek died." A return to the wartime railroad location shows the boy yelling "Daddy" as the train departs, while Tadeusz can only hold up one hand in a tentative wave of farewell. In Kraków, he later asks a bookseller—who had been an officer in the underground—what happened to Jędrek; instead of a reply, the older man counters, "What happened to six million innocent people murdered here?" Although the word "Jew" is never mentioned, *Codes* throbs with an awareness of the extermination of a race. (However, when Dr. Gross tells Tadeusz that Zofia's cousin Marian escaped from a concentration camp before going to Zofia for protection, we assume he was a political prisoner.) This awareness can even be felt when Tadeusz gazes out the window of the train to Kraków after looking at Auschwitz photos: two men are digging a grave, and one stares up at him as if they knew each other. If these are clues, an audience member of 1966 might not possess the key to unlock them. (A young man wearing a yarmulke can be glimpsed in the Kraków street montage toward the end of the film, but by 1968 the anti-Semitic purge would expel from Poland its remaining Jews.) Fifty years later, on the other hand, viewers are familiar with the shorthand of Holocaust imagery—from photos of corpses piled in concentration camps to railroad cars—culminating in the execution of large groups of people standing before mass graves.

This is indeed the central, hallucinatory tableau of *Codes*—a nightmare set in daylight, during which the boy that Tadeusz glimpsed in the train window walks calmly above the terror. Dressed in short pants and holding a lit candle as if for Communion, he traverses a snowy landscape. In a long take, the camera tracks right, as horses and then soldiers fill the frame. Tadeusz, in uniform, approaches and places the boy onto a horse, leading him over the snow. The child then looks through a window with his father, as we hear a voice-over of Zofia reciting a poem. In the climax of this sequence, the camera tracks left over a frozen tableau, following the boy, who walks outside with a priest. He passes soldiers and lines of corpses before descending to the area where a firing squad is about to execute blindfolded prisoners. While the choral voices on the sound track—and the crosses visible on top of the hill—suggest Christian victims, the mise-en-scène re-creates what we now recognize as the murder of Jews beside mass graves.

This sequence is continuous with an earlier one of the boy running amid white horses. Joined by other children, he crouches at the tracks as a train arrives, covers his ears, and yells when the train passes. A sudden cut to Tadeusz in the dining car of the train approaching Kraków implies

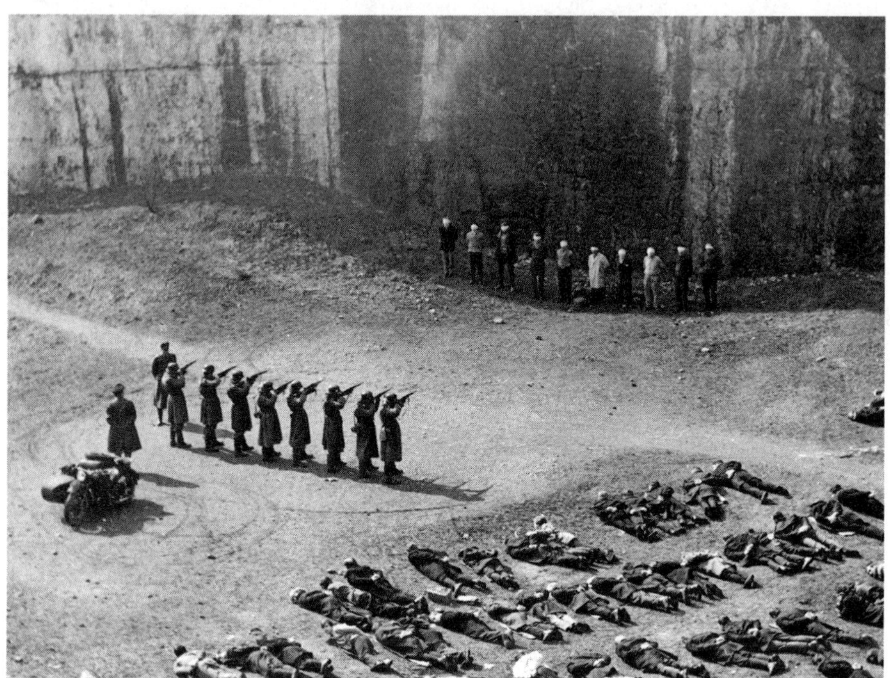

The image of a mass execution in *Codes*, by W. J. Has, 1966. Copyright © Film Studio Kadr. Photo: FN. 1-F-2648-90.

that he is remembering either Jędrek or his own exploits as a boy. Herein lies one of the film's primary unanswered questions: how much of the boy is Jędrek, and how much is Tadeusz, who would have been an adolescent at the beginning of World War I? In Kijowski's story, Jędrek is a fully realized character and a witness to the madness of World War II. But the film turns the boy into a phantom. Kijowski has Tadeusz leaving Poland at the beginning of World War II and Jędrek searching for his father in every uniform; in Tadeusz's absence, the boy seeks signs of him.[1] Has, however, transfers the quest to the culpable paternal figure seeking traces of his boy. Since Jędrek is the same age that Has would have been at the beginning of World War II, this shift of perspective provides a distancing lens onto the culpable father. (Maciej Putowski, the designer who worked on a few of his films, told me in 2015 that Has's own father abandoned him in the 1930s.)

The stream of consciousness that he utilized in *How to Be Loved* anchors *Codes* as well, but in an oneiric rather than realistic mode. If Felicja's flashbacks (during a voyage from Poland to Paris) seemed like her "authentic" recollections of World War II, those of Tadeusz (traveling from Paris to Poland)—despite their visual precision—are poetic pro-jections of his fears. They are reminiscent of Ingmar Bergman's *Wild Strawberries* (1957), whose aging protagonist (Victor Sjöström) physi-cally resembles Tadeusz (including mustache). At one point, the Swedish professor of Bergman's drama utters a line that could be about Tadeusz: "The day's clear reality dissolves into even clearer remnants of memory." There is, however, a dissonance between Tadeusz's images of Jędrek and the age of the latter during the war: he says his son would be thirty-seven today (meaning at least sixteen toward the end of the war). But the boy in the flashbacks looks like a child of ten, which suggests that Tadeusz projects onto the battlefield an innocent, prewar Jędrek . . . or an image of himself around 1914. This poetic subjectivity is the mark of an unreli-able narrator: as Tadeusz and Professor Borg visualize the past of *Codes* and *Wild Strawberries*, respectively, both films offer a partial perspective rather than historical accuracy. Through aging protagonists for whom family was not a priority, Has and Bergman explore guilt, abandonment, and a temporal entrapment: the present can't break away from the past.[2]

The war years created tension in the relationship of Tadeusz to his elder son Maciek, which Has expresses via cinematographic detail. Look-ing around expectantly when he arrives at the station, Tadeusz doesn't realize that the man grabbing a light from his cigarette flame is Maciek, nor does the latter greet him with any warmth. He says to his refined father, "We still live in a shared room," a reminder to Has's audience of the cramped conditions of his characters from *One Room Tenants* as well as *Gold Dreams*. Maciek tells Tadeusz that in postwar Poland, "everyone lived beneath his genuine value," an "unreal"—or what we might call an unrealized—existence. He remembers the war not historically (like the battlefield of his father), but domestically, "in a rented room." Estranged in time and space, the men embody a generational divide; as Tadeusz later says, "The war separated Maciek and me forever."

With Mieczysław Jahoda once again as cinematographer and Witold Sobociński (who would go on to become a leading director of photog-raphy) as camera operator, *Codes* is visually intriguing throughout. For example, the conversation between Tadeusz and Maciek in a taxi from the train station—moving around Kraków's *rynek* (main square)—remains in voice-over as we see only the rainy gray exterior, its bleakness part of the distancing via offscreen voices. Maciek recounts how they survived after his father did not come home, and says, "Jędrek was taken." Sud-denly we see the in the present-day Kraków street the boy of Tadeusz's previous flashbacks. Even if we do not yet know that this is a projection of his imagination, the image raises questions about whose perception we

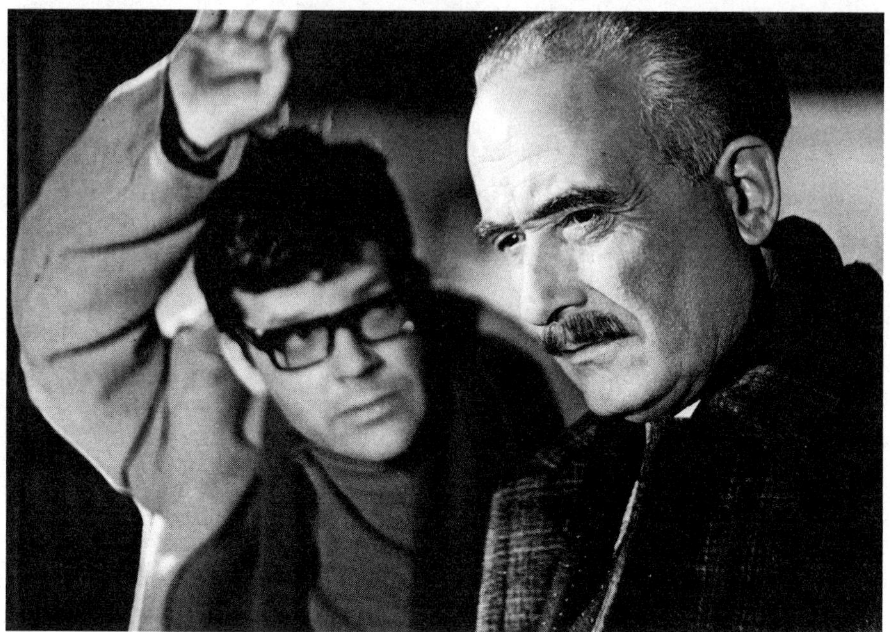

Tadeusz (Jan Kreczmar) and Maciek (Zbigniew Cybulski) in *Codes*, by W. J. Has, 1966. Copyright © Film Studio Kadr. Photo: FN. 1-F-2648-93.

share, or what to trust visually. In the next sequence, the mise-en-scène is equally expressive: Tadeusz and Maciek do not look at each other while arguing in a hotel room. The older man stands in the background, his son in foreground, neither able to make eye contact; the use of deep focus in this long take enables us to feel the literal and figurative distance between them. On the other hand, exterior shots utilize a lyrically mobile camera. For example, a subjective angle reveals crows from the boy's perspective: as they fly, the camera soars in the same circular patterns.

The sound track is evocative as well. Krzysztof Penderecki's score begins with a saxophone's lyrical wail during the opening credit sequence, consisting of still shots of Paris street life. The same music returns toward the end, accompanying bustling streets—in motion—presumably of Kraków. In the flashbacks, however, the music has an eerie, dissonant tonality that is coherent with the dreamlike settings. In the present tense—and as in his previous films—Has reminds us that music is often diegetic rather than imposed. When Tadeusz visits Dr. Gross, who is treating Zofia for depression, we hear an upbeat tune that seems incompatible with the action. As Gross turns off a tape recorder, the more "Western" music stops.[3] The scene of Tadeusz meeting Jadwiga in a café begins with a jukebox: a record is selected, and its song on xylophone will accompany their conversation about Marian, who left Zofia for her. It grounds the scene in the present tense as she tells him that Maciek loved her too—suggesting another betrayal that may have continued into the 1960s: Maciek seems to have no woman in his life besides his mother. She claims to have seen Marian killed by Germans because of Jędrek.

At the end of *Codes*, we wonder, like Tadeusz, whether he has succeeded in deciphering the codes of the past. After Maciek has taken Zofia to the hospital, Tadeusz burns the drawings Jędrek made of German soldiers. He is about to return to London when a phone call from Zofia to his hotel room changes his mind. Tadeusz seems happy to stay in Poland, to finally be of use to someone he loved, and able to fulfill a code of honor toward family. But because the last shot is dominated by a black telephone in the foreground—a visual rhyme of the opening shot of *The Noose*—*Codes* ends on a discomforting note. The hero seems tiny in the background, subject to a potentially maleficent mechanical force controlling the foreground. On the other hand, if the phone of *The Noose* provided the cord with which Kuba hung himself, the black object of *Codes* signifies a connection that could be redemptive. Given the choral voices on the sound track, the film offers a second chance for Tadeusz to be an engaged husband and father.

Despite the suggestion that Polish resisters—rather than Nazis—killed Jędrek, *Codes* was well received by critics and audiences. But within a few years, Has's work was less in favor: the criteria for successful movies returned to a depiction of national pride through a more realistic style.

✦

Chapter 9

The Doll

(*Lalka*, 1968)

If Stanley Kubrick had adapted Anton Chekhov's prose into a movie, it might have resembled *The Doll*. Has's first film in color is an opulent if dark portrait of a dour protagonist's social ascent in late nineteenth-century Warsaw. While the director wrote his own screenplay adaptation of Bolesław Prus's novel of 1899, Kazimierz Brandys—the author of *How to Be Loved*—is credited as a collaborator on the dialogue. Their backward glance at a time of upheaval is suffused with the melancholy of unrealized hopes, making *The Doll* continuous with such Has films as *The Noose* and *An Uneventful Story* (the latter adapted from Chekhov). The unsmiling hero Stanisław Wokulski (Mariusz Dmochowski) could have been the object of the first line of Chekhov's *Three Sisters*: "Why do you always look so sad?" With painterly compositions, *The Doll* traces his economic rise and romantic fall. We first see him as a waiter who plans to study science at Kiev University. But some of the restaurant's young customers play a nasty practical joke, literally preventing his ascent from the cellar to the main floor by removing a ladder. When he returns years later—having amassed a fortune in war contracts—many aristocrats are penniless and therefore ready to receive a tradesman in their homes. Most of them are already customers in his elegant shop, which is managed by his loyal older friend Ignacy (Tadeusz Fijewski).

Stanisław is attracted to Izabela (Beata Tyszkiewicz), whose father, Tomasz (Jan Kreczmar), is in debt. Although it is not clear whether he truly loves the snobbish beauty or desires an aristocratic "doll," he buys their silver and ultimately the Łęcki home, assuming it will lead to their marriage. By film's end, Izabela seems ready to accept him; however, she does a poor job of hiding her sexual relationship with her dashing cousin Starski (Andrzej Łapicki). After leaving them together on a departing train, Stanisław places his head on the tracks—but is pulled back to life

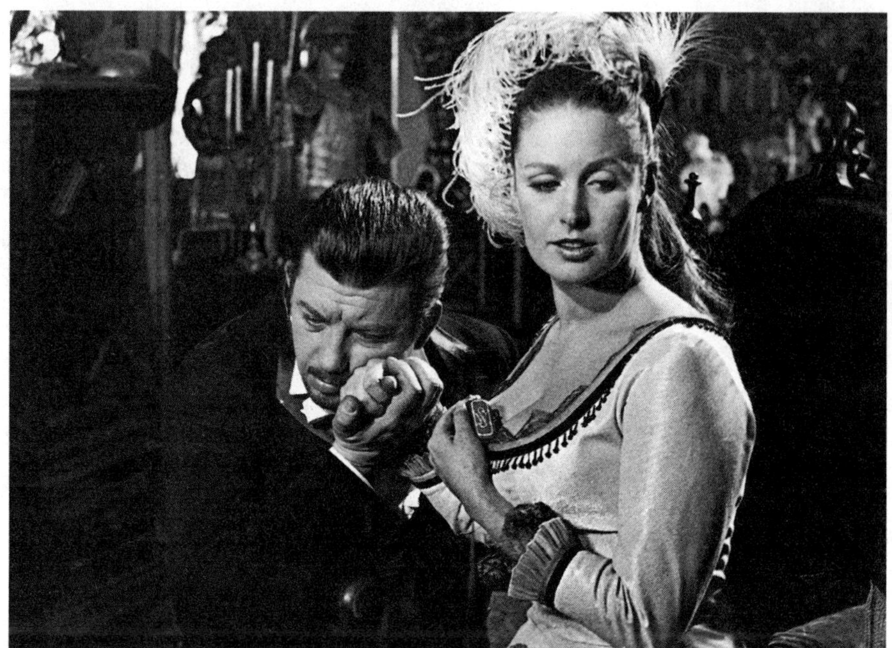

Stanisław Wokulski (Mariusz Dmochowski) and Izabela (Beata Tyszkiewicz) in *The Doll*, by W. J. Has, 1968. Copyright © Film Studio Kadr. Photo: FN. 1-F-2200-53.

by a railway worker whose brother he has helped. He returns to Warsaw to sell his shop, barely saying good-bye to Ignacy, whose solitary death—seen through a window—closes the film. While Stanisław anchors the story of a society in transition, including the rise of a bourgeois class, the sympathetic Ignacy provides the human frame. We are left with the unfulfilled potential of both Stanisław and his country. As Marek Haltof has noted, "*The Doll* centers around two worlds of conflict: the emerging Polish capitalism, represented by Wokulski and his class, and the old Polish romantic tradition. . . . This film's vast panorama of Polish society after the failed January Uprising of 1863–1864 against Russia greatly contributed to its critical and box-office success."[1]

Collaborating again with cinematographer Stefan Matyjaszkiewicz, Has introduces his cinematic translation of Prus's world via dramatic angles. They reveal economic extremes, beginning with a low-angle camera moving past a Gypsy woman singing to her baby before tracking backward to show a busy street. At key moments of *The Doll*, the dolly of the camera juxtaposes the poor who live on the margins with Stanisław dominating the center. Its motion exists in a constant tension with the stagnation of the privileged, who have pensions and see no reason to work. When Ignacy descends to the cellar of the tavern, he notices the wheel-like machine of perpetual motion that Stanisław invented, but it is now stuck. In a later scene, Ignacy instructs the staff of their boutique to place a merry-go-round in the shop window. Stanisław will find a kindred spirit in the inventor Ochocki (Jan Machulski), who wants to create flying machines; when he returns from Paris, Stanisław shows him a silver piece that floats in the air, a paradoxically magical emblem of science. Despite the stasis of mummified gentry and the circular entrapment of the poor—"They pollute the water with garbage, and then drink it," Stanisław laments about the latter—mobility is palpable in train rides as well as fluid camera movements extending from paved streets to the slums of Powiśle.

Approximately six minutes into the film, the opening credit sequence consists of a sumptuous tracking shot, traveling left past women old and young as well as dolls and garbage. Elżbieta Ostrowska has called attention to Has's "presentation of an almost entirely static mise-en-scène within a moving frame."[2] After Stanisław shows to Ochocki the silver medallion lighter than air, the camera descends to the tableau of a picnic: it tracks right, revealing Izabela in the background, dressed in white and holding a parasol, as classical music plays. In close-up, women move at a languid pace, as if inhabiting a still life, or posed like mannequins. Has's frame captures these decorously composed creatures who seem as two-dimensional as the masked women of Kubrick's *Eyes Wide Shut*. Both directors use voluptuous visuals to depict vapid and passionless people. Moreover, Paul Coates, in "Choose the Impossible," proposes that the surrealist foregrounding of objects in the frame corresponds to their fetishistic enchantment: "Melancholy and masochism are also diffused between director, character and the character type made possible by the invention of cinema, who vanishes behind objects that have more life in them than he does."[3] (Maciej Putowski, who worked on the decors of *The Doll*, provided insight into the care that Has took with visual preparation: during a 2015 interview in Warsaw, he recalled how a character not crucial to a given scene—but to the following one—would be "half-lit in preparation for the following shot.")

Has's trademark tracking shot is rhymed in two enigmatic scenes. As Stanisław follows a young redheaded prostitute from church to her home, the camera moves beneath her feet, past poor children, and down a hill. He walks on a parallel path behind her before emerging in the foreground. When they enter a decaying house, it seems like a prelude to a carnal connection; but Stanisław instead offers to save Magdalenka (Anna Seniuk) by having her learn to sew. While illustrating his typical generosity, the scene also suggests his lack of interest in sex (and we never see him fulfilled romantically). Curiously, the same lateral camera movement leads to the identical hovel toward the end of the film, but with Stanisław in the foreground walking the path of the young prostitute and his inventor friend following in the background. When they end up in the shabby room where Magdalenka offered her body to Stanisław, the formal repetition of dolly and location implies a repressed sexual component to his friendship with Ochocki.

Stanisław is depicted as more of a voyeur than a man who enjoys physical pleasures. His first act upon arriving at the room with Magdalenka is to look out from an upper window at the beggars below. (This perspective is repeated a few scenes later when he glances at beggars through the glass frame just before a friend calls him a sentimental tradesman.) At the races where the horse he purchased is competing, he looks through binoculars at Izabela more than at the winning animal. The most dramatic instance of his voyeurism is in the penultimate sequence, on a train where Starski has joined Stanisław and Izabela for their trip. Our hero goes to the bar car and, from his seat, he glimpses a window reflecting his fiancée and her cousin kissing passionately. Even after such a wrenching discovery, his reaction is muted: he asks the porter to bring him a fake telegram calling him back to Warsaw. Despite his towering stature, Stanisław's physicality is recessive, especially because Has presents him in middle age—after having made his money—rather than as an active young man. Given that he manifests less agency and passion than Prus's hero, Stanisław might be a bit of a "doll" as well, manipulated, toyed with, and ultimately abandoned.[4]

Even though Has deleted significant portions of the novel, *The Doll* conveys a vivid sense of historical time and place. (Prus juxtaposed two parallel narratives: Stanisław's story begins in 1878, while the diary of Ignacy takes the reader back to the mid-nineteenth century.)[5] At the beginning of the film, Ignacy is still under the sway of Napoléon, unhappy to hear a friend say that socialism is a greater force than Bonaparte. In his subsequent discussion of justice with Stanisław, the latter concludes ironically, "the strong flourish and the weak perish: that's justice." The protagonist has brought two hundred fifty thousand rubles and speaks of having four million more in credit in Moscow. It becomes clear that Jews are integral to his existence, as well as life in Warsaw: through his interactions with the Szlangbaum family, we see Stanisław's harmonious relationship with Jewish characters despite a pervasive anti-Semitism. When young Henryk Szlangbaum comes to his shop and says, "I'll perish in the Jewish quarter if you don't help me," he immediately hires him, and then dismisses a salesman's intolerant quip about "a smell of garlic from Polish sausage with matzo." In order to buy the Łęcki home, Stanisław asks the senior Szlangbaum (Tadeusz Kondrat, who will play the father in *The Hourglass Sanatorium*) to be his proxy. While the Jewish characters in *The Doll* are primarily moneylenders, they are nonetheless part of the social fabric and depicted rather sympathetically.

Stanisław seems tolerant and wise in close-up situations but deficient in a long-shot perspective, whether politically or romantically. His repeated claim that there will be no war is a hollow prophecy, given our knowledge that World War I approaches. When he returns alone to Warsaw at the end, he dissolves his professional relationship with the aristocrats, reminding them that their contract was only for one year. "It's a dwarfed country," he says angrily ("miniature" in the original Polish). "Some die of famine, others of debauchery, while work has to feed incompetence." But in its focus on the joyless Stanisław, the film also questions capitalism: no matter how much wealth he amasses, it neither makes him happy nor contributes to the greater good. The class system needs to be radically reshaped to do away with the despair of the poor and the torpor of the aristocracy. Because he devotes his fortune to Izabela, he is unable to support the scientific discoveries that inspired his youth. This is literalized when he gives her the precious floating metal that tantalized Ochocki. (She later loses it.) Had he not been obsessed by this ideal of female and upper-class beauty, Stanisław might have incarnated a true hero, the new man of a democratizing middle class that alleviates poverty while injecting more humane values into the foppish nobility. (Although the film does not foreground his ancestry, and we know that his family lacked money, Stanisław is of noble birth.)

A hint of his own innate nobility can be seen in the sequence of his duel with a comic baron who is totally dependent on his butler. Feeling insulted by the nobleman at the end of the horse race, Stanisław demands satisfaction. At the actual confrontation, he succeeds in shooting the baron's pistol so that it smacks his cheek, knocking out some teeth rather than killing him. Over a glass of champagne, they make peace. The code of conduct—offense followed by a duel (in Polish, *pojedynek* suggests one-on-one)—seems as hollow as the French phrase that begins the shoot-off, "Messieurs, en avant" (Gentlemen, forward!). Indeed, the smatterings of English and French throughout *The Doll* are reminders of the Western European culture that represent upper-class Polish aspirations: for example, Izabela and Starski flirt in English in front of Stanisław, assuming he does not understand them. But he says to her at the end, in accented English, "I have learned your true feelings toward me. Farewell."

Like most of Has's films, *The Doll* boasts a sound track of nuance and emotional effect. Wojciech Kilar's score in a minor key captures the lyricism as well as the tension palpable in the images, often with the counterpoint of tinkling music that one might associate with a dollhouse or merry-go-round. During the opening credit sequence, one note trembles, heightening the off-kilter coexistence of the rich and the homeless. As in many of Has's films, the music is occasionally diegetic. For example, during the final extended tracking shot that follows Stanisław and Ochocki, we hear an accordion song and then see the musician playing this instrument in the street. When they get to the dilapidated room, a violinist plays in the background while Stanisław says, "Fate makes damned fools of us sometimes" before he exits. The characters are surrounded by music that suggests an aesthetic order beyond their reach.

The sound of crows toward the end links *The Doll* to Has's *Uneventful Story* fifteen years later. Much like the professor of Chekhov's story, Stanisław expresses an existentialist awareness when he says quietly to himself, "a senseless struggle, for nothing." Elżbieta Ostrowska sees Has's profound distrust of progressive change as distinct from the dominant paradigm of Polish postwar cinema, which conceives of history as a linear goal-oriented sequence of events.[6] Indeed, the perpetual motion machine invented by Stanisław is a perfect emblem for Has's vision of both society and the individual psyche: rather than moving forward, it can only turn back in on itself.

✦

The Hourglass Sanatorium

(*Sanatorium pod klepsydrą*, 1973)

It took Has five years to make *The Hourglass Sanatorium*. He wrote the screenplay, adapting Bruno Schulz's story collection *Sanatorium under the Sign of the Hourglass* (published in 1937). Schulz, a Jewish writer known as Poland's Kafka, was murdered by a Gestapo officer in 1942 for stepping outside the ghetto of his Galician town. Given the film's striking and pervasive Jewish imagery, it can be seen as a phantasmagoric layering of at least three time frames—the pre–World War II past of Schulz's stories; the Holocaust; and a postwar Poland haunted by the ghosts of dead Jews.

Visually and aurally, Has interweaves the theme of time. The very title in Polish, *Sanatorium pod klepsydrą*, has a double resonance: *klepsydrą* means not only the hourglass device but also an obituary notice. The film thus takes place under the sign of death. *The Hourglass Sanatorium* is indeed disorienting and nightmarish, less a linear narrative than a composition of internal rhymes—stories within stories—containing the logic of dreams. Moving through dreamscapes of dilapidation, the constantly tracking camera of Witold Sobociński conveys a rich darkness. Given the prevalence of a self-conscious low-angle camera as well as dissonant sound design, meaning emerges through surreal visual and aural juxtapositions.

We follow Józef (Jan Nowicki), who travels by train to visit the sanatorium where his father, Jakub (Tadeusz Kondrat) is dying. He discovers a crumbling space surrounded by gravestones whose mysterious doctor (Gustaw Holoubek) keeps patients in a suspended state between living and dying. He lies down in the dank room where his father sleeps. Does Józef dream what we then see? He embarks on an internal voyage in which his adult body is the only thing that does not change. When he enters the past, his mother speaks to him as if he were still a child; Hasidic Jews pray and dance in the market where his father has a textile shop,

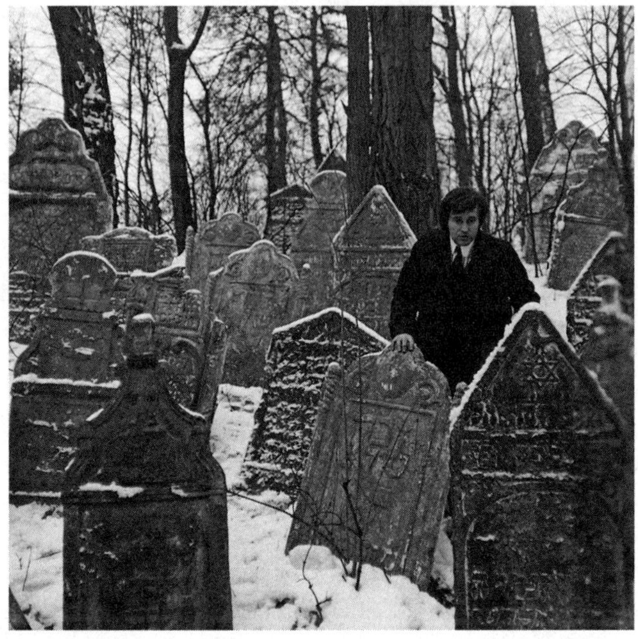

Józef (Jan Nowicki) amid Jewish gravestones on the grounds of *The Hourglass Sanatorium*, by W. J. Has, 1973. Copyright © Film Studio Kadr. Photo: FN. 1-F-1870-400.

and men wear the heads of exotic birds. Often accompanied by Rudolf, a bespectacled schoolboy, Józef moves through bizarre landscapes: he is hunted by colonial mercenaries as well as haunted by mechanical creatures representing historical figures. Finally back at the sanatorium, he is able to speak to his dying father before Józef exits into a giant cemetery covered by burning candles.

The Hourglass Sanatorium begins with an exterior shot of a raven's silhouette flying left in slow motion, while the camera tracks right. In addition to this lateral movement, the camera pulls back, emphasizing depth as it reveals that our perspective has been through a train window framing the sky. It moves further back to show the train's pervasive darkness and decay. Seen from an extreme low-angle perspective, religious Jews are seated, but it is not clear if they are sleeping or dead. We glimpse a child on the bottom left of the frame; an empty wheelchair on the right; a bare-breasted woman sleeping, a clock, and sacred Jewish Torah scrolls. The film's action begins only when Józef is awakened by a blind conductor who announces the next station as his destination. This opening introduces key elements that will be developed throughout the film. The wide-angle lens prepares for the perspective of a child, while reminding us that we are an audience looking up at the screen and subject to entrapment because the ceilings bear down on characters. Moreover, the distorting lens invokes a subterranean—or hellish—perspective, consistent with Józef's often disappearing underneath a bed or a table, crawling amid debris into a new space. The unseeing eyes of the conductor prepare for the disembodied eyeballs that Józef later finds, as well as an oculist sign hanging in the street: while suggesting an omniscient perspective (as in *The Great Gatsby*), its circular frames are empty—conveying the absence of a divine gaze—as Józef watches Jews fleeing, clutching their suitcases while men on horseback charge behind them. As the story ends, the doctor places the uniform of the train conductor on Józef, who seems to be suddenly blind too. The film's last shot is a descent into darkness, a return to the underworld beneath a cemetery.

Surrealist imagery informs *The Hourglass Sanatorium*, leading us to question what we see. Józef looks down through the sanatorium window early in the film: first he glimpses a schoolboy, then two dogs, and finally his own arrival (much like the end of *The Saragossa Manuscript*, where Alfons sees his own body receding into the distance). In a kind of rewind, Józef watches himself opening the huge doors again, but this time the boy Rudolf helps him, and the doors open to an outer expanse of lush nature. Józef lifts a dark veil, revealing the image of his mother (in a mirror): she treats him as if he were still a child. (The covered mirror invokes shivah, the period of mourning following a death.) In the square outside their apartment, masks of exotic birds cover the men's faces. The surreal images continue as he sees the blind train conductor carried aloft on a chair (accompanied by the sound of whipping), with elephants moving alongside. Bianka—a lovely young woman whose huge bed is outdoors—tells Józef about her mother, who dreams specters. Here, the word *zagadka* ("puzzle," already invoked in *The Saragossa Manuscript*) seems to refer to the film itself. Moreover, when Józef says, "It's so muddled," his father responds, "One has to make a grammatical analysis of it." But the rational mind is insufficient to comprehend the detours of *The Hourglass Sanatorium*. When Rudolf says to Józef, "You depend on me," does he represent our hero as a boy? Józef falls into a jungle as the camera tracks left, revealing skeletons of animals. "Remains" of a different kind populate an abandoned villa, where people appear to be frozen in poses. Mr. de V. explains these mannequins to Józef, including "a young man in whom much hope was placed, but who was lost to masturbation": the bespectacled youth looks like an older Rudolf, which suggests an image of Józef as well. Surrealist imagery abounds when, amid eyeballs and cobwebs, he finds his father in bed, in a white sheet. Filled with the birds (some with maggots), the attic seems like an aviary. Józef then descends to his mother, who sends him to his father's store with a tray containing two apples and a glass of tea. But the seductive Adela stops him, placing on his tray the severed head of a woman. Józef is then arrested, blindfolded, and taken back to the sanatorium. He is now awake, and his father is well. For Has, the film screen serves as a dream space, a locus of poetic associations that give shape to the protagonist's internal landscape.

True to Schulz's drawings, the women in this space are highly sexualized caricatures with breasts on display. The first person Józef glimpses at the sanatorium is an attractive nurse, her top buttons undone. In the scene where sleeping Jews awaken in the marketplace, he climbs a ladder and sees through a window the taunting redhead Adela. When the cemetery is revealed toward the end of the film from the sanatorium window, prostitutes wear little (apart from cigarette holders). Linking sex and death, these figures are reminiscent of the exaggerated female creatures of Fellini's films, projections of male fear and desire. (The sexual ambiguity toward the end includes Józef's realizing that an overweight man talking to him has the large breasts of a woman.) Bodies are objects to be looked at rather than touched, much like the images of food and water that tempt Józef. After arriving at the sanatorium, he takes a piece of cake from the restaurant but does not get to eat it. In one of the scenes of Jewish prayer, when he sits at the long table and hungrily eyes the whole fish served by Adela to the Jewish men, it is devoured before he is able to take a bite. And when he tries to get water from a spout in the corridor of the sanatorium, all that falls into his kettle is a few drops. (One is reminded of the line quoted by Felicja at the end of *How to Be Loved*, "dying of thirst beside a fake stream.") Amid sensorial overload, Józef remains physically unsatisfied in every way.

The sound design is equally rich throughout, beginning with the eerie tones of the first shot (including buzzing and whispers), followed by crows when Józef walks from the train through a snowy landscape. In the sanatorium, we hear the agitation of cymbals as well as voices, and later water dripping. The atonal score by Jerzy Maksymiuk not only expresses an off-kilter universe but also includes klezmer melodies in the last sequence. Moreover, the words uttered are often incantatory: Rudolf has exotic stamps pasted into a book and recites the names of places—"Borneo," "Calcutta," "Patagonia"—much like Józef pronounces "Abracadabra" to animate the mechanical facsimiles of historical figures. He also yells for "a horse" before horses appear.

Has once again explores temporality, especially through cobwebs, which give shape to the passage of time. In the first scene, a clock is one of the train's "passengers," anticipating the dangling pieces of the watch peddler who brings Józef into the scene of Jews praying: each holds a burning candle in the twilight, another objective correlative of time passing, reminiscent of the candle in the train conductor's lantern box (which he wears around his neck). As Isabel Robinson has noted, "The dual nature of the candle's flame resonates well with the temporal duality that Has explores. The flame is almost impossibly delicate, transient, completely lacking in substance. Its entire existence can be ended in a literal pinch. And yet coexisting with this fragility is the power to consume all organic matter, a destructive ability that very few entities share. It is not a coincidence that time is one of those few entities." Another crucial observation is provided in a website essay by Steve Mobia—namely, that there is no visible hourglass in the film: "The only oblique reference to it occurs in Jacob's bird attic. While he's busy building nests, he talks about disengaging the grain of time as he sprinkles birdseed down. The sand grains of the hourglass are compared to birdseed, thus death to regeneration."[1] On the other hand, he calls attention to the numerous clocks and watches: "Unlike an hourglass that pours in one direction until the glass is empty, a clock creates a sense of eternity as the hands round the circle to begin their journey again. There might be no external evidence of a clock stopping until the hands cease to move. This hidden fate is conveyed in Joseph's uncertainty until the end as to whether his father is alive, dead or dying." Time is less a linear process than a circular dimension, especially when Józef becomes the blind train conductor at the end. As Rudolf shows him stamps from exotic places, Józef says he feels déjà vu: "Don't we already know the landscapes through which we will move?" Has invokes the possibility of both temporal loops and parallel universes. As Mobia proposes, "Rudolph, the boy, opens the door from the other side and Joseph enters. The blockage has disappeared and the entrance seems to lead to a garden or forest. Has has visually set up a context for two simultaneous stories—one happening with Joseph and his father in the sanatorium and the other with Joseph following Rudolph into a world of nature."

As the doctor, Gustaw Holoubek—the star of numerous films by Has—seems to be the director's mouthpiece: "We turned back time," he tells Józef. "Your father's death hasn't reached here yet . . . This all boils down to relativism . . . We reactivate past time including the possibility of recovery." Similarly, the blind conductor tells our hero, "Plain facts are chronological, lined up on a thread . . . There are sidetracks of time . . . Maybe we're on a dead-end track, blind," before suggesting that Józef start again under the bed.[2] At the end, Józef says about the sanatorium, "It's regurgitated time, second-hand time"—a line taken directly from

Schulz's story, whose narrator speaks of "used-up time, worn out by other people, a shabby time full of holes, like a sieve. No wonder. It is time, as it were, regurgitated—if I may be forgiven this expression: secondhand time."[3]

John Updike says in the introduction to the stories, "Bruno Schulz was . . . one of the great transmogrifiers of the world into words,"[4] celebrating how "writers in a world of hidden citizens work with an excited precision, pulling silver threads from the coarse texture of daily life. The hypnotized gaze upon local particulars turns objects into signs . . ."[5] Reading Schulz's original tales alongside Has's film is an illuminating process, especially given how rarely this director also functioned as the sole screenwriter. The deletions and amplifications of the prose suggest an even darker labyrinth than Schulz created. Much of the film is actually taken from the story "Spring," including Rudolf, Bianka, and Mr. de V. (her father). The translation by Celina Wieniewska is lush, leading the reader to feel the heightened—even hyperbolic—sensitivity of the narrator: "Then at about ten o'clock the sun appeared like a luminous smudge from under the swollen body of a cloud, and suddenly among the tree branches all the fat buds began to shine and a veil of chirruping uncovered the now pale golden face of the day. Spring had come. . . . The whole park became shamelessly pimply, and all the trees came out in buddy spots, which burst with the voices of birds."[6]

The "Caribbean" elements of Has's film originate in "Spring," whose narrator intones the exotic names of Barbados, Labrador, Trinidad and describes a wax exhibition that came to town, including a resurrection of Maximilian: "It was not a miracle, but a simple mechanical trick. Suitably wound up, the Archduke held court in accordance with the principles of his mechanism, graciously and ceremoniously as he had done when alive."[7] The first-person singular narrator of this story continues in "Sanatorium under the Sign of the Hourglass," beginning with the first scene in a train; however, Schulz makes no mention of Jews, clocks, cobwebs, or death. The conductor is not blind but "looking at me with washed-out eyes."[8] The double glass door of the sanatorium is open. Only when Józef meets Dr. Gotard does Has cite Schulz's prose directly: "We have put back the clock. . . . Here we reactivate the past, and all its possibilities, therefore also including the possibility of a recovery," says the doctor.[9] If the characters of Has's films rarely eat, Schulz's Józef at least gets to taste pastries when he ventures out in the market square. And if the movie ends with the blind hero roaming a landscape of graves covered by lit candles, the story culminates in Józef's taking the train away from the sanatorium: he becomes a shabby railwayman, living on the train, but with sight.

Has's alterations of Schulz's stories connect the film more deeply with *The Saragossa Manuscript*. As Columbia University student Chantel Clark proposed in an unpublished essay of May 2016, "The Sanatorium is not dissimilar to the Inn—functioning as both time machine and dream engine . . . Temptation (possibly at the hands of the devil) from an otherworldly portal, and the impending death of a parent living on borrowed time in a phantasmagoric sanatorium, test Alphonse and Jozef's devotion to their fundamental beliefs." If they also challenge the viewer's grasp of time and space, it is partly due to the cinematographic dislocation. In a Polish television interview of 2004, Witold Sobociński revealed details such as stretching the 35 mm frame by 2½ millimeters, having the camera track and pan from the same position, and using different color palettes for each time frame: "Although green is rarely used for death, it made me think of garbage, and we therefore used it for the last sequence," he recalled.[10]

Adam Garbicz's review of Has's movie in *Film Quarterly* notes the importance of Galicia for Schulz as well as the director: "Formerly an Austrian crown-land and after 1918 again a part of Poland, Galicia was a most curious country. Someone who does not have firsthand experience of this conglomeration of dignified poverty, vivid intellectual temperaments, Jewish enterprise, and picturesque handicrafts will not understand fully the Galician spirit—unless he penetrates through *The Hourglass*. For one value of the film is beyond question: the inspired accuracy of description of the writer's world, a world which was to vanish irrevocably during World War II. This aptness of description is not fortuitous. Has is a Galician by birth, by temperament, and by choice, and his tastes, particularly visual, have their roots in the *fin de siècle* artistic avant-garde of Cracow."[11] The visual style of *The Hourglass Sanatorium* is indebted to a few Has collaborators, including art director Andrzej Haliński and production designers Andrzej Płocki and Jerzy Skarżyński (who, together with his wife, Lidia Skarżyńska, designed the costumes): the couple previously performed these roles on his *One Room Tenants*, *Partings*, *The Saragossa Manuscript*, and *Codes*. Along with the cinematography, their decors lead Garbicz to suggest, "The resurrected Galicia has the colors of a painted corpse, at once more vivid and more morbid than reality, like the flushed face of a consumptive."[12] During an interview in Warsaw in June of 2014, Andrzej Haliński recalled the challenges of re-creating a Jewish town, as well as Has's delight in fabrication: "He wanted to have everything built on the set, not real locations," Haliński told me. "He found a street in Tarnów, in the southeast of Poland, called Żydoska [Jewish] Street. 'Promise me it will look like a set,' Has insisted about the real

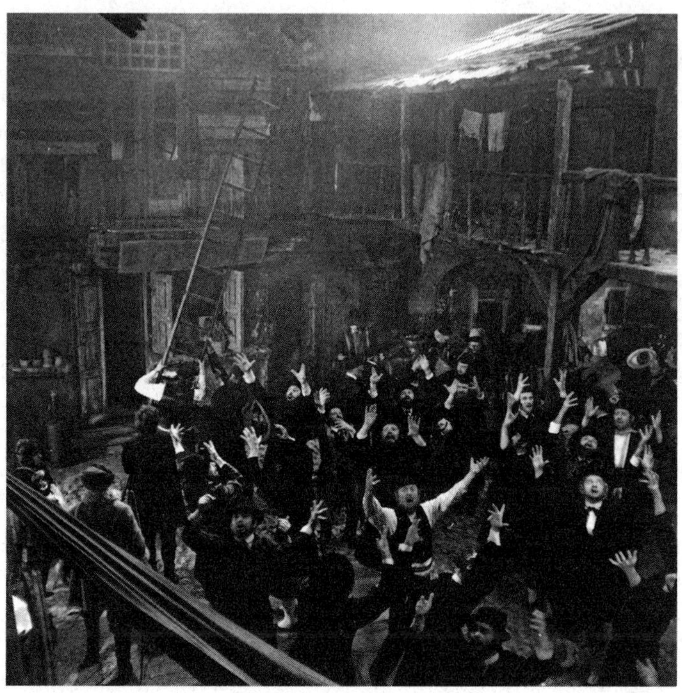

Hasidic Jews pray and dance in *The Hourglass Sanatorium*, by W. J. Has, 1973. Copyright © Film Studio Kadr. Photo: FN. 1-F-1870-147.

street." For the decor of the synagogue, Haliński remembered painting "the whole synagogue with biblical scenes, enlarging Jewish letters," and added that "actors from the Warsaw Jewish Theatre came in makeup." In 2015, Maciej Putowski, who served as set decorator, pungently invoked Has's direction to these actors: "Don't over-Jew it."

While resurrecting prewar Galicia, the film contains a biblical resonance, with the protagonist being Józef, son of Jakub. He is even asked by a guard if he dreamed the dream of the biblical Józef. But the allusion is perhaps ironic. The ladder leading to Adela's room provides an ascent only into voyeurism and carnality. Later, Adela bites into the apple that was meant for Jakub, and then Józef takes a bite as well. (When Józef enters a circular structure where he will encounter Haitian soldiers, there is no ladder, and he descends via rope.)

Given the prevalence of Jewish iconography in *The Hourglass Sanatorium*, Has seems to be performing his own "Abracadabra," breathing magical cinematic life into a long-gone world. Wearing an antique fireman's hat, Józef goes out into the courtyard, where a man awakens— uttering the Yiddish word *meshugener* (lunatic); Hasidic men sing, dance, and pray ebulliently as the light of dawn enters the frame. Józef raises his arms too, but as an observer rather than participant. He moves through the Yiddish-inflected market of *handel* (bargaining) and *tumul* (noisy activity), now sporting a more traditionally Jewish hat. Huge rectangular windows topped by circular ones invoke a synagogue. From the market, the camera tracks left as Józef and others unfold a red carpet onto wet ground for the "Three Wise Men" arriving. (Ironically, they have gold skin and debate the merits of credit versus cash.) A more authentic depiction of Jewish tradition follows, as we hear the Hebrew prayer of havdalah (the end of the Sabbath) at dusk with candles; a table is set with challah; men toast one another with "L'chayim."

The train of the opening sequence connotes something darker in 1973 than in 1937. Carrying Jews who look almost dead, it is a prophetic image of the means of transport used by the Nazis to move their victims to concentration camps. As Mobia has noted, "*The Hourglass Sanatorium* is a film not only of a father's death and a son's remorse but of the death of a culture. Jacob's textile shop opens onto a large synagogue and becomes the hub of the town's social activity. Mourners holding candles pray before what feels like a final feast, the last gathering before the great scattering that would take place as the Jews either emigrated or were murdered by Nazis." The crumbling space of the sanatorium is really a cemetery and—with Jews depicted only as ghosts—conveys the sense of Poland as the graveyard of an entire people. In a post-Holocaust context, even the remark of Jakub—"We love books for the moment they soar like a phoenix . . . although they return to ashes"—seems to refer to those who wrote the books, especially Bruno Schulz. "If the film departs visually from the tone of Schulz's prose," David Melville has proposed, "it does so only by making the characters and setting explicitly Jewish in a way the books do not. . . . Schulz expresses his Jewish identity largely through suggestion and subtext."[13]

Was Has drawn to Schulz's stories because his paternal grandmother was allegedly Jewish? In Warsaw, Łódź, and Kraków, I tried to ascertain the director's own possible Jewish ancestry, especially given Wikipedia's claim that his father was born into this religion and the inclusion of Has in the 2010 book *Żydzi polscy* (Polish Jews).[14] Has never identified publicly as a Jew—which would have been a death sentence during World War II—but he often chose the work of Jewish writers to adapt—for example, Schulz and Kazimierz Brandys. (Wanda Has, his widow, mentioned that he planned to film an adaptation of Jarosław Iwaszkiewicz's novel of 1934, *Red Shields* [*Czerwone tarcze*], but abandoned it after being pressured to substitute Gypsies for the Jewish characters.) Moreover, his films convey an exile that is as much internal as external—the sense of a marginalized outsider with no place of his own.

Some of the people I interviewed in Poland in 2014 did not think he had Jewish ancestry, while his former student Sławomir Kryński—now head of directing at the Łódź Film School—recalled, "He never acknowledged or denied being Jewish." But a few confirmed his affection for Judaism. According to Andrzej Haliński, "He definitely felt like a nonbeliever, but he considered himself to be Jewish. In my opinion, his mother was converted too. At our first dinner at the film club, four of us were sitting together. He asked me, using a Hebrew word, '*Amchu?* Are there many of us on the set?' I asked what this word means. The answer was, 'Are you of my tribe?' I didn't 'pass this exam.'" Haliński (whose wife is Jewish, although he is not) added that he left Poland in 1968 because he didn't want his son to grow up amid anti-Semitism.

When I returned to Poland in 2015, I was able to search in Kraków's national archives. There I found the official birth and baptismal certificates of the director's father, Stanisław Has, from 1892 (the same year in which Schulz was born)—including the names of his paternal as well as maternal grandparents—which affirm Catholic rather than Jewish ancestry. These records make it even more intriguing that Has was so deeply and consistently drawn to Judaism. Wanda Has termed him a Judeophile as well as a Kabbalist and Freemason and said that he learned Hebrew in order to read the psalms. "He showed me a book from 1968: he had signed a letter defending Jews and was arrested. He loved that culture," she insisted and recalled going to Israel with him in 1993, when he taught for a month in Jerusalem. "Those who were against him called him a Jew anyway," said Maciej Putowski. And Małgorzata Burzyńska-Keller, who had been Has's student, recalled in 2015 an anti-Semitic remark made when he was shooting *The Hourglass Sanatorium*: Bohdan Poręba, the filmmaker (and hard-line Communist Party member), allegedly quipped about the director and his crew, "Has, Has, Hasids."

She wrote her master's thesis about *The Hourglass Sanatorium* and its celebration of Jewish traditions. "I came to him in 1986, and we were close," she told me in 2014 in Łódź. "He was raised Catholic and was a philo-Semite. We had things to say to each other, and things to be silent about." She praised Has for making "the only Polish film with no mistakes about Jewish religion," recalling such details as the precise candles for Yizkor (memorial) or havdalah. She believes he was not merely fascinated by such rituals but in fact created an elegy for the lost Jews of Poland. "I brought him amulets from Israel, which he would hang up

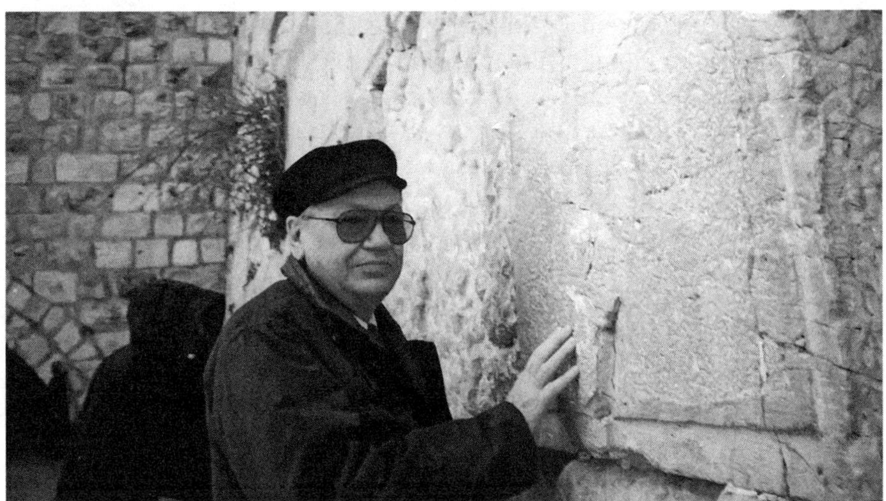

Wojciech Has at the Western Wall in Jerusalem. Photo taken by Wanda Has in 1993 and provided by Małgorzata Burzyńska-Keller.

to ward off evil spirits. And he loved Gołda Tencer's music," she added, referring to the Polish singer known for Yiddish songs. A few weeks after we met, she provided a photo of Has at the Western Wall in Jerusalem (taken by Wanda Has in 1993).

For Józef, finding his Jewish father is equivalent to dying himself. From a basement window, he sees people running with their suitcases and joins them in a prescient image of the Holocaust. At the end, now blind, he climbs up to lit candles near gravestones (unable to see his mother in the left corner). The camera tilts down to darkness, suggesting a purgatory or hell. While these closing images are merely evocative in the abstract, they become profoundly meaningful in the specific context of the annihilation of Polish Jewry during World War II. The experience of watching *The Hourglass Sanatorium* through this prism is analogous to attending a production of *Waiting for Godot* in Yiddish. In September of 2014, the New Yiddish Rep presented Samuel Beckett's play as part of Origin's First Irish Theatre Festival in New York. This "tragicomedy in two acts" took on a new and radically authentic life in the language of Jewish irony and resilience. Given that the play was written in 1948, hearing it in Yiddish anchored the characters and situations in a post-Holocaust awareness: in act 2, "All the dead voices . . . Where are all the corpses from? A charnel-house," seems to refer specifically to the extermination of the people who spoke this very language, rendering Beckett's characters as Holocaust survivors.

It is not surprising that Polish authorities did not appreciate *The Hourglass Sanatorium*. Some were uncomfortable with Has's sympathetic foregrounding of Jewish life, a mere few years after the government's 1968 expulsion of approximately thirty thousand Polish Jews. Others interpreted the decaying sanatorium as a symbol of the run-down institutions in Poland. As Nick Hodge wrote in the *Kraków Post*, " 'Did you know sir, that your dream has been noted and severely criticized in the highest places?' So Józef is informed whilst being arrested by a soldier at the end of the film. This comes straight from Schulz's 'Spring', but such elements, accentuated by Has in his own script, seem endowed with a fresh resonance under the director's baton."[15] Although Has was not permitted to officially submit *The Hourglass Sanatorium* to the 1973 Cannes Film Festival, a print was smuggled to France, where the jury (presided by Ingrid Bergman) awarded it the Jury Prize.

✦

Chapter 11

An Uneventful Story

(*Nieciekawa historia*, 1983)

Like *The Noose, An Uneventful Story* stars Gustaw Holoubek as a hyper-lucid man who senses both the meaninglessness of life and his proximity to death. Has wrote his own screenplay adaptation, thickening the late nineteenth-century sadness of Anton Chekhov's short story with post-war despair. Although Hłasko and Chekhov provide disparate points of departure for films made twenty-five years apart, the unity of tone resides in Has's formally vibrant treatment of existential lassitude. As the center of these cinematic variations on a theme, Holoubek incarnates an alcoholic in the former and a professor of medicine—addicted to cynicism and alienation—in the latter. The sheer acuteness of his ironic glance at self and world makes him a compelling subject in both films. The professor's voice-over narration replaces much of the dialogue—this unnamed protagonist barely answers his wife when she speaks to him—and brings the viewer into complicity with his disillusionment. He has little patience for the mediocrity or hypocrisy that abound in the provincial town (repeatedly described as gray) where he has taught for thirty years. *An Uneventful Story*, unfolding over approximately two days and in just a few locations, moves ineluctably toward a renouncement of living.

Even if Has does not name his hero, we will identify him as Chekhov's Nikolai Stepanovich. His internal monologue calmly but caustically observes his existence, which appears to consist primarily of insomnia, diminishing mental dexterity, lack of love for his wife Weronika (Anna Milewska), and disdain for the pettiness around him. While he seems fond of his daughter Liza (Elwira Romańczuk), he barely tolerates her foppish suitor Gnekker (Janusz Gajos), an impresario with affectation. Nikolai is ungenerous outside his home as well: when a student walks in his path on a narrow plank above a muddy puddle, he pushes the youth—who stumbles off. He applies overly high standards to another pupil, who has flunked his exam, chiding him for an absence of medical vocation. Later, he is dismissive to an advanced student seeking a dissertation topic. The only person for whom he manifests genuine affection is the actress Katia (Hanna Mikuć)—an orphan he and his wife raised as their own child—who has returned to town. During his visit to her home, she acknowledges painfully that she has no talent. When Nikolai's wife beseeches him to confirm Gnekker's claim of a wealthy family, he sets off for the suitor's hometown but first goes to an abandoned inn near the train station. Having stayed there decades earlier, he takes the same third-floor room he once occupied—even though it is being renovated—rather than the finished first-floor one offered. Katia follows him there and asks for advice or encouragement; he dismisses her with a hopeless if incisive monologue in a long take (addressed to the camera): because he cannot see an overall pattern to his existence—something beyond daily actions—all it takes is a good cold to undo his mental balance. After Katia departs, he lies down on the bed, palms under his head, facing a window in the heart of the screen. Because it is reminiscent of the internal frame of *The Noose* as well as of *How to Be Loved*, the window seems fatal. Through the bars of the bed, we see Nikolai—a prisoner of his own intelligence and irony—probably waiting to die.

The film opens with the same lateral camera movement that brought us into the space of *The Noose*: it tracks right, passing the artifacts of a home—albeit far more opulent than the room of the alcoholic Kuba—lightly caressing surfaces until it stops at a clock. Nikolai's internal monologue begins precisely with this image of time graphically represented. Suddenly we hear a young female voice—only later will we recognize it as Katia's—expressing suffering because of other actors. This verbal "flash forward" locates us firmly within Nikolai's stream of consciousness. His own voice returns when a lit candle is blown out, preparing for a visual as well as metaphorical darkness created by Nikolai. We then see him for the first time, in a mirror. Has's double narration—visual and aural—juxtaposes the subjectivity of voice-over with the "objectivity" of mise-en-scène: the camera meticulously records the details of late nineteenth-century Kalisz (a Polish area belonging to Russia), from the white quill that mockingly reminds the professor of his writer's block to the samovar from which tea is elegantly poured.

Has orchestrated Andrzej Haliński's production design with the work of cinematographer Grzegorz Kędzierski, creating—in color—a palette of rich darkness. (The camera operator was Piotr Sobociński, who became Kieślowski's cinematographer for two of the *Decalogue* segments as well as *Three Colors: Red*. Kieślowski's final feature seems like a contemporary

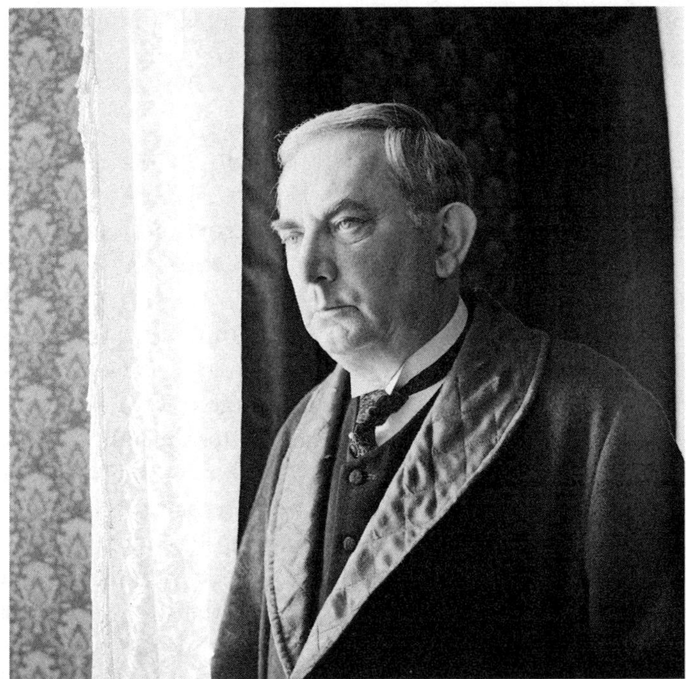

Gustaw Holoubek in *An Uneventful Story*, by W. J. Has, 1982. Copyright © Film Studio Kadr. Photo: FN. 1-F-1939-104.

revision of *An Uneventful Story*: a caustic older man and a lovely young woman have a mutually beneficent connection by the end.) Kędzierski would continue as Has's director of photography on his next three features.[1] At times, the composition expresses alienation: for example, a wide-angle shot of Nikolai seated at the dining table exaggerates the distance from his wife, daughter, and guest Gnekker. (As the others happily eat their puree, he pushes the soup away after one taste.) Moreover, the window is once again a dramatic threshold between the passive man inside and the outer world: Nikolai often looks at leaves burning below the pane, or at crows above.

The camera's low-angle track of the branches mirrors his gaze, especially when we return to a shot of his eyes looking up. The crows that intrigue him assume increasing importance in *An Uneventful Story*: a brief scene of crows killing two baby birds suggests a Darwinian universe with little inherent meaning. It is painful to watch the chicks dying in close-up, the head of one falling near the other. Is this a naturalistic representation of the real world? Could it be that the nest fell out of the tree, and the crows are mourning the loss of their babies? Or is it a projection of Nikolai's morbid speculations? Because the next shot is of Katia rather than Nikolai, the crows' murderous actions seem to exist in their own right.[2]

The shriek of these creatures punctuates *An Uneventful Story*, a counterpoint to the chimes of clocks and church bells. (Their cries are heard in the opening sequence—followed by distinct sounds of a clock ticking, a doorbell, and the creaking floor—before the crows get louder.) The film's intricate sound design resounds with chaotic nature on the one hand and a temporal order created by human beings on the other, crystallized by the shot of a clock caught in the flash of lightning during a storm. As in Has's other films, the muted clanging of clocks in homes or the sonorous echoes of church bells outside mark the passage of time—the hours that, for Nikolai, repeat only meaningless rituals. After the lightning, his monologue quotes from Aleksey Arakcheyev, "Nothing good in the world can exist without the bad, and there is always more bad than good." Nikolai concludes, "There is no reason to go on. One has to see the years I've lived as lost." Similarly, the score by Jerzy Maksymiuk is simultaneously lyrical and unsettling. From the film's opening, the string-based melody is in a minor key; later, one note is held on violin while the piano plays notes both melodic and dissonant. Nikolai even expresses his existence in terms of music: "My life seemed like a beautiful composition. But I'm spoiling the finale," he says to Katia.

Has's interpretation of Chekhov's tale—which is known under various English titles, including "A Boring Story," "A Dreary Story," "An Uneventful Story"—is faithful only to a point, compressing events of a few months into what seem like a few days.[3] Neither provides details about the protagonist's health: "I have no more than another six months to live," says the sixty-two-year-old narrator without elaboration. (A mistake in the English subtitles is identical to one in *The Hourglass Sanatorium* for Józef's father: "I'm busy" is less resonant than the Polish *Nie mam czasu*, "I have no time.") While the film's transposition maintains the outer frame of a professor of medicine who has lost his taste for life, Has's choices foreground the stylistic and thematic concerns that mark his cinema. He added windows (including Nikolai seeing the burning of leaves), the street scene of his blocking a student's way on a plank, and his taking the same hotel room that he occupied years before. Monologue was externalized into dialogue. While Nikolai expresses increasing alienation from wife and daughter, Chekhov does not suggest that he loves Katia in any way but paternal. One is tempted to read connections between author and character since Chekhov noticed his own illness in 1889, the year he wrote *An Uneventful Story*. But the connections between Has and Chekhov are plentiful too: both refused ideological or didactic art, preferring the descriptive and the suggestive, raising questions rather than declaring answers. And, as Alicja Helman has pointed out, "When the film was made, both Has and Gustaw Holoubek (the actor playing the part of the professor) were the same age as Chekhov's protagonist; the spectator realizes that Holoubek portrays not only the professor but also the author of the book on which the film is based and, to some extent, himself. He delves into the problems of old age with painful sincerity and cruel self-realisation."[4]

Given his invention of the crows scene, Has replaces Chekhovian nostalgia with Darwinian doom. While he retains the Russian writer's tone of regret, there is a greater sense of tragic waste. *An Uneventful Story* is an autumnal film, beginning with the burning of leaves that the professor frequently watches outside his window. Death figures prominently, including a cadaver to be studied in the university lecture space, a mention of Katia's dead baby, and Nikolai's musing, "Fate has given me a death sentence."

As the professor enters an empty bar, the film's last sequence begins with the sound of church bells chiming eight times—reminiscent of *The Noose*, where Kuba hangs himself at 8:00 A.M.—and rhyming with eight chimes struck at the beginning of *An Uneventful Story*. Mirroring Kuba's rejection of Krystyna, Nikolai has refused Katia's plea that he go to a sanatorium to be cured. It ends in a room that will likely be the protagonist's final destination: as in Has's first feature, not only a window but also a ladder features prominently. An online review of 2007 calls attention to the omnipresence of the ladder, "visible through the window in the doctor's home, sometimes being used to pick apples and . . . at the end, too, like a metaphysical warning draped in the commonplace. But, what does the ladder warn against, what does it mean? Perhaps the ability to ascend, to reach higher; or, conversely, the danger of falling, the risk in 'reaching out.'"[5] Although Nikolai says to Katia, "I'd like to live another few years," he has brought his medical bag, presumably containing whatever he might need for an offscreen suicide. He tells her of his *pragnienie* (literally, "thirst") for something that cannot be fulfilled. Like most of Has's protagonists, Nikolai speaks of food but ingests little. If his internal monologue during the family meal at home expressed a futile longing for simple cabbage soup and dumplings, this is the precise dish that the servant brings to his room. But since Katia enters just as he is about to taste it, he ignores the food. Nikolai doesn't get to eat literally, perhaps because he is fed up figuratively.

The sense of waste might be related to the director's own bitterness during the early 1980s. Because Communist authorities allegedly blocked his filmmaking efforts in retaliation for showing *The Hourglass Sanatorium* at the Cannes Film Festival without their approval, *An Uneventful Story* turned out to be Has's first feature in ten years. When I interviewed Kędzierski in Warsaw in June of 2015, he connected the protagonist's "psychic death" with Has's lengthy period of creative inactivity: "He wrote *An Uneventful Story* right after *The Noose*, when the existentialist theme was popular. But by 1983, it was connected to the silence imposed on him." Kędzierski even likened the director to Nikolai in the sense that "he was a master from whom one could learn, but not an educator." Recalling that it was his first major feature as a director of photography, he mused that—after nine years away from directing—Has was like a beginner too: "From today's perspective, I think he doubted whether he still had the sharp claw of his earlier masterpieces. Only after he saw the test shots was he reassured. But beware of how present copies of the film are degraded, no longer capturing the darkness of the soul."

Chapter 12

✦

Write and Fight

(*Pismak*, 1985)

Write and Fight is a period drama set primarily in a prison cell during World War I. But Wojciech Has's adaptation of Władisław Terlecki's novel (published in the same year the film was made) can also be appreciated as a meditation on imprisonment and imaginative freedom in Communist Poland. With a focus on Rafał (Wojciech Wysocki), the young writer to whom the title alludes, it is deeply related to Has's previous work. (The Polish word *pismak* literally means "scribbler.") Like the director's quietly anguished protagonists from Kuba in *The Noose* to the professor of *An Uneventful Story*, Rafał seems like a man out of time as well as place. He is a restlessly modern iconoclast who has been arrested for blasphemy and ridiculing the establishment in his satirical magazine *The Devil*. Reminiscent of the aspiring writer of *One Room Tenants*, Rafał must share a room with others, lacking privacy while succumbing to illness. His fellow prisoners are Szpicbródka (literally, "beard tip"), a safecracker zestfully played by Zdzisław Wardejn, and Sykstus (Jan Peszek), a former priest arrested for killing his mistress's husband. The prison is depicted as a limbo similar to that of *The Hourglass Sanatorium*: since its inmates have not yet been formally charged, they languish in incertitude, periodically interrogated by the wily investigating judge (Gustaw Holoubek).

Quarantined in the hospital wing, Rafał occupies a bed—and a disintegrating space—familiar from a few Has films: we see a bright window in the heart of a dark frame and hear dripping water (suggesting decay from an unseen source) as well as the chiming of an offscreen clock. Collaborating once again with the gifted cinematographer Grzegorz Kędzierski and production designer Andrzej Haliński, Has explores the physical limitations that define creative possibilities. Because Rafał falls ill with typhus, a few scenes express his feverish imagination rather than a verifiable reality. In Kędzierski's words, "The biggest challenge for me

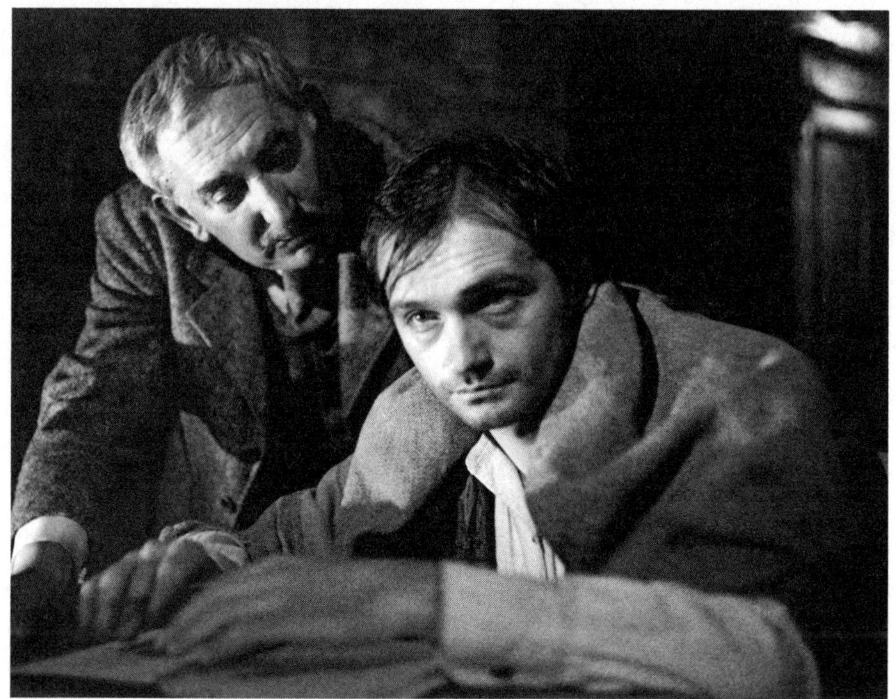

Gustaw Holoubek and Wojciech Wysocki (as Rafał) in *Write and Fight*, by W. J. Has, 1984. Copyright © Film Studio Kadr. Photo: FN. 1-F-1799-3.

as the camera operator was creating two completely different labyrinths which were overlapping in a Has-like manner—a claustrophobic world of the prison walls was merging with the wall-less internal labyrinth of the protagonist."[1]

A prologue depicts the battlefield of World War I, but primarily via stasis: like the cellmates we will encounter, soldiers are trapped in fearful anticipation before they receive the order to advance from the trenches. When these Germans finally charge into battle, a young man falls, at which point *Write and Fight* cuts to an interior space: Rafał is introduced in a mirror. The reflection creates a distortion on the right side, connecting the self-awareness of the hero with that of the filmmaker. The shot prepares for Rafał's later conversation with the prison doctor, who proposes, "What is truth? The need to constantly distort reality." Like Has's other work, *Pismak* invites a distinction between the *real*—what can be perceived—and the *true*, which can only be intimated. For example, Rafał's photo is taken in the interrogation room, an objective and unambiguous capturing (in full light) for the purpose of identifying him.

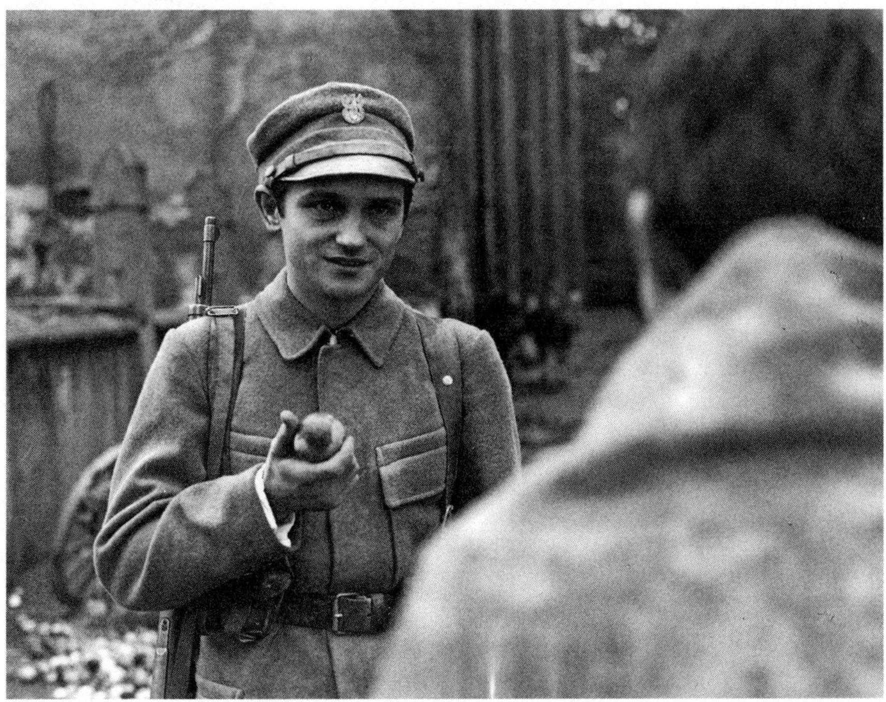

Rafał (Wojciech Wysocki) sees a soldier with his own face in *Write and Fight*, by W. J. Has, 1984. Copyright © Film Studio Kadr. Photo: FN. 1-F-1799-1.

But the most memorable shots of *Write and Fight* are dramatic close-ups of the protagonist in a train, with an intermittent light externalizing his tense state.

The distortion caused by lighting is related to Rafał's creative process of reshaping what he sees into a verbal narrative. After he arrives in the cell that he will share with the two inmates, shadows often prevent us from seeing his entire face. The dappled darkness heightens his privacy as well as secrecy—Rafał observes everyone, taking notes for the book he is writing—while externalizing his struggle for clarity. This is especially true after he collapses with typhus, his sweaty face half in shadow. At the end of the film, Rafał is the last to leave the prison, with a blanket over his frail shoulders. In the garbage-strewn street, he talks to a young soldier who bemusedly eats an apple; under a cap, the youth's face resembles Rafał (it is indeed the same actor). Since *Pismak* represents the story Rafał has been composing, most of the characters are indeed projections of his fragmented psyche. He is first and foremost a prisoner who realizes his growing vulnerability: he could be charged with crimes to which he bears no connection. (The investigating officer claims that a gun found in his apartment was the weapon that killed two people in a terrorist attack.)

Second, beyond his satirical drawings and articles, Rafał is an aspiring novelist, whose notebook scribbles are visualized by Has as waking dreams. The most stunning and sustained scene begins with a meal in the cell: while Sykstus and Rafał eat bread and thin soup, a feast from a restaurant is delivered to the safecracker. This engenders an outdoor scene as we hear the offscreen laughter of ladies: the safecracker and his actress friend (Marzena Trybała) are seated with Rafał at a table. Via such extravagant fabrications, *Write and Fight* self-consciously raises questions about the function of art and the slippery identity of the writer. Two crucial scenes unfold during Rafał's ride in a train car with girlfriend Maria (Gabriela Kownacka); after she pulls shut the curtains on the window, he says of his upcoming book, "The subject is connected to how it is told. First I wanted to be the main character; that was a mistake. It's best when the author remains hidden, observing from the shadows, narrating through someone who is unrecognized." It is surprising to suddenly see another man in the compartment, resembling Rafał but wearing glasses. Our hero tells the stranger (Jerzy Zelnik)—who is also a writer—that the world needs to be described. His face lit only intermittently, the traveling companion disagrees, arguing for the supremacy of dreams: "The world seeks truth there, in dreams," he insists. "The world exists only within us." The mysterious writer is on his way to America, where, as he puts it, he can presumably be "true to myself, to be sure of who I am. . . . I have to kill my own weaker nature." As the conversation ends, Rafał's head reclines to the left, and he awakens in his cell. Was this a memory or a dream? When we return to the same train compartment later in the film, the bespectacled writer seems to have already completed his distant voyage, concluding that life is similar in America. Maria asks if the trip was worth it. "Yes, because I couldn't have been homesick had I stayed here," he replies. And he claims that a quality being lost in Poland might be retained in America—dignity. (Perhaps it's relevant that Władysław Terlecki [1933–99], who wrote *Pismak*, had been a literary editor for Polish Radio and then worked unofficially in the 1970s for Radio Free Europe.)

The self-referential quality of *Write and Fight* continues in the sumptuous outdoor scene with the safecracker: Rafał states, "My method of writing is like photography: I show the exterior, leaving the inner self to be discovered by those who hold the photograph." At this moment, Has revels in his own beautifully deceptive "exteriors": the camera tracks laterally, embracing Gypsy dancers as we hear a lyrical folk song (one that Emir Kusturica would use effectively in the wedding scene of *Time of the*

Gypsies). He reveals the decor as an emanation of the hero's imagination: the music continues as Rafał writes in his cell, a reminder that he is composing this scene from his imagination. Equally important is how Has enriches the sound track, heightening our awareness of what is just beyond the frame.[2] It begins with the sounds of gunfire and wind as German soldiers wait in the trench before advancing. We hear the clock when he is summoned to fill out papers, as well as chimes after the investigator enters, and the scene of the firing squad ends with the sound of crows. The music, composed by Jerzy Maksymiuk, is once again filled with both tension and lyricism.

A third identity for Rafał—and part of being an artist—is that of voyeur. Like the director and his previous heroes, Rafał is drawn to windows. When he first arrives in the cell, he goes to the barred glass and peers at the departing carriage. Later, he looks down on the prisoners circling the yard murmuring Catholic prayers. The third time is after he awakens in the hospital ward: he walks haltingly to the window and sees corpses being placed into coffins below. Maria then visits him: standing in front of the window, she is associated with the outer world that is still denied to Rafał. This internal frame remains a barrier between exterior and interior space. The fourth iteration is toward the end, as Rafał climbs up to a window and sees men leaving the prison. It engenders a scene that begins as "real" but increasingly belongs to Rafał's febrile imagination. He is blindfolded after a priest blesses him and stands before a firing squad. Removing the blindfold as shots ring out, he wakes up.

The window is one of numerous internal frames in *Write and Fight* that foreground representation—the "description" that Rafał claims necessary in art. These include a risqué photo album of women in provocative poses that the safecracker shows him in their cell: like Rafał's anticlerical sketches, it constitutes another kind of "forbidden" imagery. He prefers this to the other reproductions Szpicbródka presents to him—namely, drawings of insects "that resemble the world of people," in the safecracker's words.

Judaism is a fourth identity for Rafał. The possibility that he is Jewish emerges in the film's second scene, when he is told he has been accused of subversive activity for satirizing the church: he asks if the complaint against him was in Hebrew, ironically wondering aloud, "Did the Lord write it in Hebrew or Latin?" When he is first interrogated in the prison, the functionary asks his religion; he says none. "Impossible. Are you Catholic? Orthodox? Lutheran?" In the absence of these, the functionary says (and writes), "Jewish then." Later, in the cell, the safecracker looks over Rafał's shoulder and asks, "You're reading from right to left? I didn't

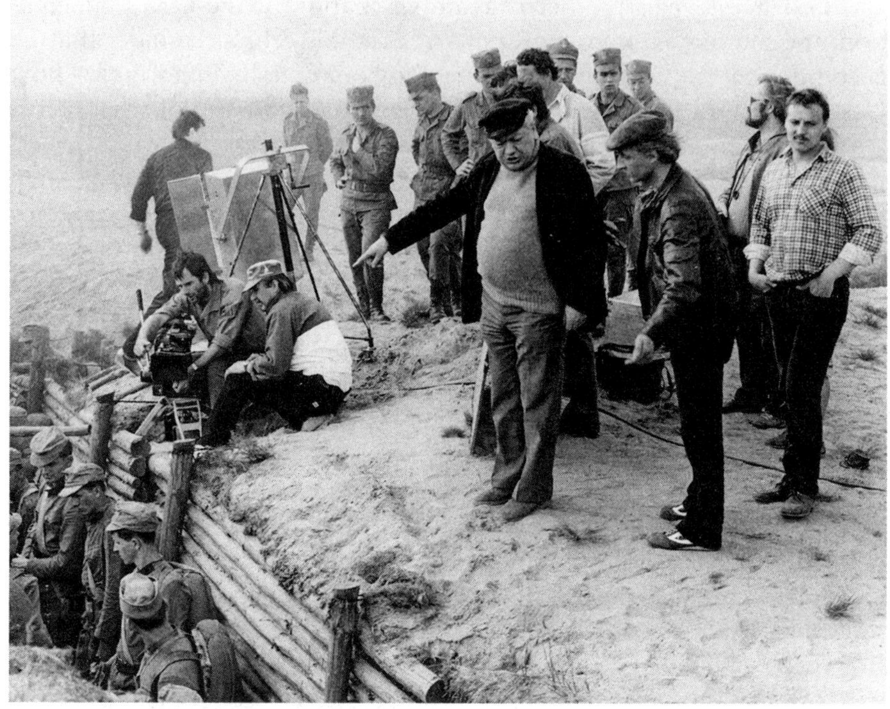

The filmmaker directing *Write and Fight*, by W. J. Has, 1984. Copyright © Film Studio Kadr. Photo: FN. 1-F-1799-93.

know you were a Jew." Rafał neither affirms nor denies this assumption. (In fact, when the prison doctor subsequently asks whom he offended, Rafał answers, "A favorite of rich Jews and conceited bishops.") To his cellmate's remark, "You Jews have a great sense of sin," he replies, "I never thought about it . . . I lost my faith long ago." The safecracker then admits to sometimes saying the Ten Commandments in his dreams and proceeds to recite them in excellent Hebrew—which Rafał translates and identifies as a prayer for the traveler. (Kędzierski confirmed that Szpicbródka was Jewish too and added that Rafał was writing from right to left because he did not want others to understand his scribbling.) The same lines return at the very end of the film: as Rafał leaves the prison and walks into the heart of the frame, the voice-over of the priest says, "Thy will be done/Our God and God of our forefathers/Let us go forth safely/And proceed on our way in peace/Let our journey be untroubled/And let us reach our goal in good health, joy, and peace." If the hero is indeed Jewish, he bears an even stronger relationship to Józef in *The Hourglass Sanatorium*—both suspended in a dank building, surrounded by death, and fabricating vivid visions. The death of his grandfather begins Rafał's story (not unlike that of Magdalena in *Partings*), while Józef tries to reach his own father before he dies.

Twice in the film we hear a line that resonates with more than one meaning in Polish. *Wróć do siebie* is not simply "Go back to your place" but "to yourself," as if identity is not separable from one's physical space. The writer in the train has been to America but returned to Poland after being homesick. Can a writer be himself in a different language? Was there too much freedom abroad for an Eastern European? Is censorship—which informs much of *Write and Fight*—necessarily the enemy of creativity? Maria tells Rafał that the new issue of their satirical magazine has been published, but with cuts due to censorship. Later, the investigating judge laments that Rafał's articles praise anarchy and chaos; and when he asks Rafał to name possible subversives with whom he met, he refuses. He is therefore detained without being charged, a situation with obvious parallels in the Poland of the 1980s. Made four years before Solidarity finally brought free elections to Has's native country, *Write and Fight* can be seen as a nuanced critique of a vulnerable system that silences and imprisons those it fears. Paradoxically, the lack of political freedom functions as a spur to creativity, whether for Rafał early in the twentieth century or Has toward its close: censorship incites a coded and therefore heightened poetic exploration of identity as well as society.

Chapter 13

✦

Memoirs of a Sinner

(Osobisty pamiętnik grzesznika przez niego samego spisany, 1986)

Has's fascination with the fragmented male psyche assumes spectacular visual form in *Memoirs of a Sinner*, set in eighteenth-century Scotland. The screenplay, by Michał Komar, was adapted from James Hogg's novel of 1824, *The Private Memoirs and Confessions of a Justified Sinner*: the narrator is a tormented soul who encountered his nefarious double. This psychological thriller—which predated *Dr. Jekyll and Mr. Hyde* by sixty-two years—was ripe for cinematic translation, and in Has's hands, the Scottish novel became a vibrant questioning of doppelgänger and destiny. His gothic costume drama has two narrators, the voice-over of Robert (Piotr Bajor), whose semiliving corpse is exhumed in the opening scene, and a mobile camera that prowls landscapes external as well as internal. Robert tells the grave robbers of his past as the illegitimate son of Rabina (Hanna Stankówna) and the pastor Prudencjusz (Janusz Michałowski). Her vulgar, wealthy husband, Logan (Franciszek Pieczka), fathered first-born Gustaw (Jan Jankowski) in a moment of rape that led her to curse the child at birth. Robert is incited by the apparition of an unholy twin (in body, voice, and clothing) to reclaim his birthright by killing his biological half brother. Although he is repulsed and tries to resist, Robert begins to change—drinking wine, spying on hedonistic brother Gustaw, and acting less kindly to his parents. The Satanic double returns in the guise of a "Stranger" (Maciej Kozłowski), now dressed like (and sporting the facial features of) Logan. While claiming, "Everything is already destined," he persuades Robert that he is fated to kill Gustaw. This manipulative Stranger sows doubt and unleashes violence while denying freedom or responsibility. The distraught Robert seems to kill his brother, followed by matricide and patricide; unable to stop his double from committing the horrific acts, Robert finally chooses suicide to end his torment, piercing the heart of his "other" with a blade.

Memoirs of a Sinner opens with images and sounds familiar to viewers of Has's work. From a low angle and in long takes, the tracking camera of Grzegorz Kędzierski follows men who plunder graves. The nocturnal landscape yields a hand and then the open-eyed corpse of the titular sinner. Robert slowly comes to half life, telling his tale with raspy breaths that engender luscious flashbacks. The score, by Jerzy Maksymiuk, again originates in a tense held note, later amplified by bagpipes, zither, and French horns during a hunting scene. In tandem the sound track and camera work create a paradoxically menacing lyricism. The self-conscious tracking shots prevalent in films like *The Doll* give equal plausibility to scenes of "real" and "dream" experience (insofar as anything in Robert's flashbacks could be deemed actual). And even when the camera is static, the movement within the frame is dynamically meaningful. For example, in a scene toward the film's end, the men dance laterally, in between two attractive women: Robert moves into the center, then out—replaced by the Stranger—sharing the frame in a mobile manner.

Has develops the visual self-consciousness through scenes of explicit voyeurism. After Robert's first temptation by his own image, he follows a young couple frolicking by the water. Gustaw and an attractive woman begin making love but then notice him and flee: the mere gaze of Robert has deprived them of their idyllic interlude. Moreover, two scenes involve a spyglass. At his mill, Logan looks through this object to see his wife playing a harp outdoors, the pastor beside her, and the enlarged belly under her ornate dress indicates she is pregnant. This voyeurism is repeated when the Stranger goes to this very window later in the film, peering through the spyglass in the same direction at a harp-playing woman who may be Rabina's double.

Mirroring assumes numerous shapes, both literal and metaphorical, throughout *Memoirs of a Sinner*. There is first the obvious resemblance between Robert and the identical twin, who says, "I'm your brother." Second, the Stranger (as he is identified in the credits) seems to be simultaneously an emissary of Satan and Robert's other half. But there is a curious tertiary connection between the double and Robert's stepfather, Logan. When Robert II first takes leave of the hero, he turns in the same way as Logan before mounting a horse. The Stranger and Logan are not only dressed identically but also have the same long curls and prominent nose. The Stranger stands at the window and looks through a spyglass at a woman playing the harp, quoting the scene of Logan doing the same. At the end, the Stranger places his own jacket and hat on Robert so that the latter evades arrest: from a distance, he looks just like a young Logan. With this confusion of birthright, Has suggests that the amorally lusty

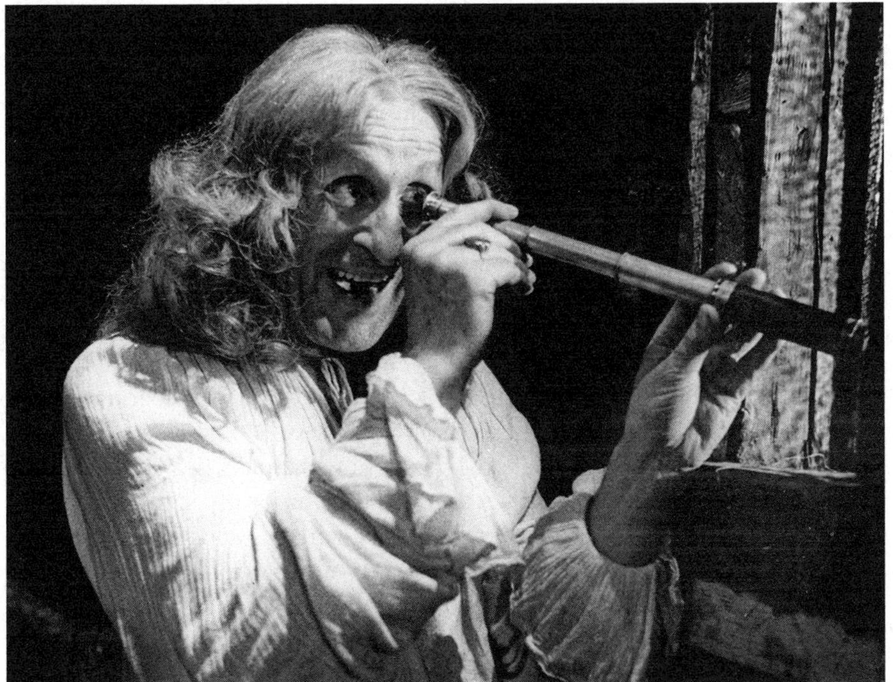

Logan (Franciszek Pieczka) in *Memoirs of a Sinner*, by W. J. Has, 1985. Copyright © Film Studio Kadr. Photo: FN. 1-F-2205.

Logan is in a sense Robert's "real" if not biological father, and that suppressing his more libertine impulses has resulted in an unhealthy situation.

The film interweaves a host of dualities. The duality of life and death begins with the open-eyed corpse coaxed to speak. At one point, Robert II tells Robert, "You are dreaming," a reminder of Has's predilection for juxtaposing oneiric scenes with "real" ones. Bisexuality is part of this thematic thread, especially when Logan finds his wife in the arms of an undressed woman before he rapes her. Moreover, Robert's long orange hair and soft features suggest an androgynous protagonist rather than an identifiably male figure. While women flirt with him, he manifests little romantic passion. When he initially visits the inn frequented by Gustaw, two attractive wenches (Katarzyna Figura and Anna Dymna) circle him. Later, at an opulent banquet, the same women are elegantly attired guests, still sexually playful in their treatment of him. Laura (Ewa Wiśniewska), an older redheaded woman, seems to have more than one face. She is glimpsed in Rabina's position playing the harp. Later, Robert kisses her shoulders, whereupon her face becomes that of his mother. When he places his hand around her neck for a moment, it is Rabina who moves away into the background. After an ellipsis, we understand that she has just been murdered.

The tension between good and evil is established by the first conversation with the doppelgänger, who counters Robert's "faith" with the notion of "sin begetting sin." This relates to the friction between human freedom and a determinism articulated, ironically enough, by the Stranger. (According to David Cairns, "Hogg's satiric purpose in extending the Calvinist principle of predestination . . . is slightly obfuscated, and Has uses the tale more as a device to create unease and intrigue and . . . beautiful images, richly colored, hazily soft-focus, and with a slyly gliding camera which sometimes imparts an almost three-dimensional effect, aided by the different hues of light pooling his sets.")[1] Robert being blindfolded with a white handkerchief by laughing women is a replay of the identical scene of Logan in this position. The temporally sightless Robert invokes Oedipus, whose fate is to have sex with his mother and kill his father. No matter how much he strives to avoid the riddle of the Sphinx, Oedipus cannot escape his destiny. Has thus draws on Greek tragedy as well as the Bible, presenting the devil as a shape-shifting tempter who urges Robert to take what is his brother's. The result escalates from fratricide to patricide.

When Robert says to Laura at their first meeting, "It's a puzzle where I've seen you before," we are reminded of how this word, *zagadka*, was uttered in *The Saragossa Manuscript* and in *The Hourglass Sanatorium*. Perhaps like the incorporation of jigsaw puzzles into the contrapuntal narrative of *Citizen Kane*, it crystallizes Has's labyrinthine structure that leads the viewer to actively piece together fragments of meaning. The last sequence of *Memoirs of a Sinner* is laced with images that invoke his previous period masterpieces. After Robert goes outside, the background reveals a man hanging from a gallows. Reminiscent of not only *The Saragossa Manuscript* but *The Noose* and *One Room Tenants* as well, the corpse also foreshadows Robert's suicide. In the last scene, lit candles dot the landscape as the low-angle camera tracks laterally, following the walking ghosts, which include Robert and his parents. He kneels before the flames like Józef, the blinded time traveler of *The Hourglass Sanatorium*, also half-dead.

Because Robert ultimately cares most about saving his manuscript—he calls it "my private diary" when snatching it away from the Stranger—he can be connected to Rafał, the hero of *Write and Fight*. (All four of Has's last movies feature a voice-over narrator.) Even more than his imprisoned predecessor, Robert has succeeded in recording his own tale, which is

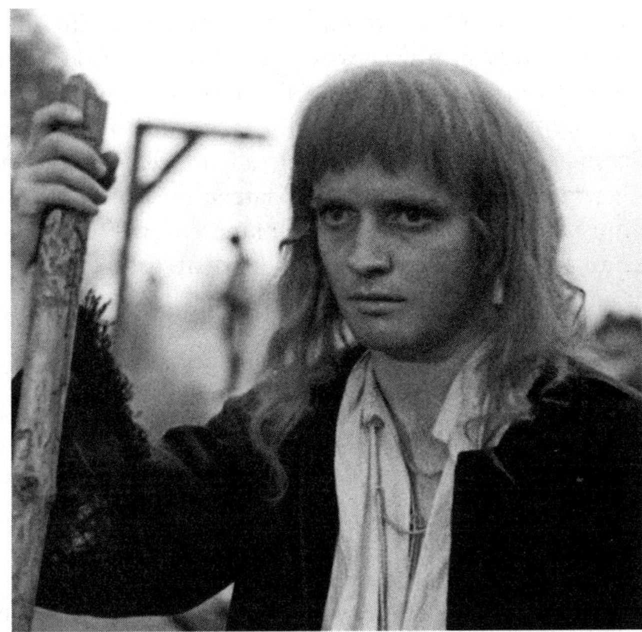

Robert (Piotr Bajor) in *Memoirs of a Sinner*, by W. J. Has, 1985. Copyright © Film Studio Kadr. Photo: FN. 1-F-2205-10.

then repeated in voice-over: the book is a testament to his identity, despite his mental state being under siege. (Hogg's book ends with an editor's statement claiming that the manuscript was exhumed from the author's coffin.) The circular structure of *Memoirs of a Sinner* brings us back to the beginning, as Robert finishes his tale. "Woe to whoever tampers with my manuscript," he warns. Bad luck plagued the real-life production history, not unlike Shakespeare's "Scottish play." According to David Cairns, "In 1988, celebrated Scots filmmaker Bill Douglas prepared a screenplay adaptation, but died before he could get it made. I was present when the producer suggested it as a suitable project for Lindsay Anderson to take over, but Anderson himself died not long afterwards. A fresh script has recently been created by crime writer Ian Rankin and James Mavor, but has yet to go before the cameras. Those involved are advised to beware falling objects, shadowy assassins, sudden illnesses."[2]

Has's film seems to have been made without grave mishaps. Its voice-over narration retains and respects Hogg's perspective, even as the Polish director makes the Scottish tale his own. *Memoirs of a Sinner* illustrates a perceptive remark made by David Melville: "The past, for Has, was more than another country. It was, at once, his act of defiance and his means of escape."[3] Has refused to make contemporary films and could be intransigent with those in power who wished to help him. He lived by a tough-minded ethical code, exemplified in Janusz Kijowski's recollection of how he was admitted to the Łódź Film School in 1974, when Has was already teaching there. Anne Guérin-Castell cites Kijowski, who became one of Has's protégés: he learned years later that Kuszewski—dean and head of admissions—had crossed his name off the list of applicants because he had participated in 1968 student demonstrations. Has told his superior, "You can cross him off the list, as long as you then cross me off the list of professors."[4]

Alicja Helman acknowledges *Memoirs of a Sinner* as one of the late-career films that "affirm the absolutely exceptional position Has occupies in the history of Polish cinema." Although the title of her essay is "The Masters Are Tired," she praises his singular voice: "Unlike the productions of many Polish film-makers, whose artistic choices and decisions were to a considerable extent determined by changes in political life and culture, Has seems to be largely apart from such influences. In his films he has created a surreal, visionary world, and has developed a specific style and poetic for which he has found neither partners nor competitors in Polish cinema."[5]

Chapter 14

✦

The Fabulous Journey of Balthazar Kober

(*Niezwykła podróż Baltazara Kobera*, 1988)

Has's final film was *The Fabulous Journey of Balthazar Kober*, aka *The Tribulations of Balthazar Kober*, a French-Polish coproduction and a curious hybrid. Set in Germany during the sixteenth century, this adaptation of Frédérick Tristan's novel unfolds against the backdrop of inquisition, plague, and glimmers of freedom sparked by the invention of the printing press. In baroque tableaux of what Has called a "dreamwork," he follows Baltazar (Rafał Wieczyński), an impressionable teenager, alchemist, and orphan.[1] His voyage is one of initiation in thought and faith. A budding theologian with a stammer, he is drawn to at least three inspirations: ghosts of his family, a group of lively actors, and an alchemist-mentor (Michael Lonsdale, voiced in the Polish version by Gustaw Holoubek). The low-angle tracking camera of Grzegorz Kędzierski once again provides a unity of tone, whether crawling through foliage at the beginning or gliding into the underworld toward the end. Permeated with candle flames, the lush cinematography of *The Fabulous Journey of Balthazar Kober* connects Has's last work with the stylistic extravagance of his previous films.

Although a plot summary and scene description can hardly convey the texture of this motion picture, they might provide a useful sketch. Accompanying a shot of dense foliage, the voice-over of a young woman asks to be taken to "the happy land, from which no one returns," and a male voice replies, "Yes, to the land of the living." (The lines may be from the film's last scene, suggesting a circular structure like that of Has's earlier work.) The archangel Gabriel appears in the landscape to sixteen-year-old Baltazar and tells him to enter the purifying fire. As the youth complies, the credits unfold on the flames. At home, Baltazar tells his little brother Gaspard the rather fantastic tale that he just returned from Jerusalem, where he prayed with the prophets. He enters the theological seminary but is mocked by students because of his sensitivity and ability to communicate with other worlds. After his father dies, the young hero is surrounded by spirits of the dead, including the fallen angel Flamand. Riding a donkey on his way back to Dresden, Baltazar encounters the performer Pappagello, who brings him to his troupe of actors. There, he meets Rosa (Adrianna Biedrzyńska), a beautiful lute player. But when he awakens the next morning on a meadow, he is alone. Baltazar arrives at an inn, where Mathias (Zbigniew Zamachowski) befriends him. He learns about the printer Zimmermann, hunted by the Inquisition and protected by the actors as well as the alchemist Dr. Frederick Cammerschulze. Baltazar becomes the disciple of the latter, who says he will teach him printing and how to find God in all things. The apparition of his mother (Emmanuelle Riva)—who died when he was a child—visits Baltazar. Vulnerable to the Inquisition, he is furtively transported from the city in a coffin, part of a procession of plague-ridden corpses. When the ghosts of his loved ones tell him they led Baltazar to the master Cammerschulze and the actors, he replies, "Maybe you're a figment of my sick imagination." At an inn, Baltazar recognizes three seminary students, one of whom stabs him. After finding the now-dead seminarians in a cellar, he descends to hell, hoping to have their souls moved to heaven. When he awakens, the three students are alive, and Cammerschulze tells Baltazar he must journey alone to Venice and find refuge with Strozzi. Assisted by Mathias, he locates the cleric, who tells Baltazar that his master made a deal with the devil and returned to Germany (for a show trial of the Inquisition "to frighten those who think freely") in exchange for Baltazar's safe passage. Our hero eludes the Inquisition by giving money to a cardinal, at a residence that seems to be a brothel where beautiful topless women bathe. Baltazar is reunited with Rosa, whose glistening face emerges in a cave: she goes off with him riding a gondola that floats through the dark mist amid candle flames dotting the water.

As in *The Saragossa Manuscript*, Has uses the narrative structure of theme and variations, returning to the protagonist waking from sleep to different versions of events. Whether depicting a nightmare or a parallel universe, this purposeful ambiguity leads the viewer to identify with Baltazar's remark, "I can no longer distinguish dream from reality." As the director explained, "In Frédérick Tristan's novel, I have been deeply moved by the conflict between Balthasar and the world which surrounds him," defining the hero's universe as "invisible, spiritual, . . . inhabited by angels, defunct loved ones, creatures and events risen from dreams and from a reality interwoven with phantasms" (from the French press kit of *Fabulous Journey*). The "rewind" element emerges halfway through the film, when we return to the spectacular shot of windows shattering above

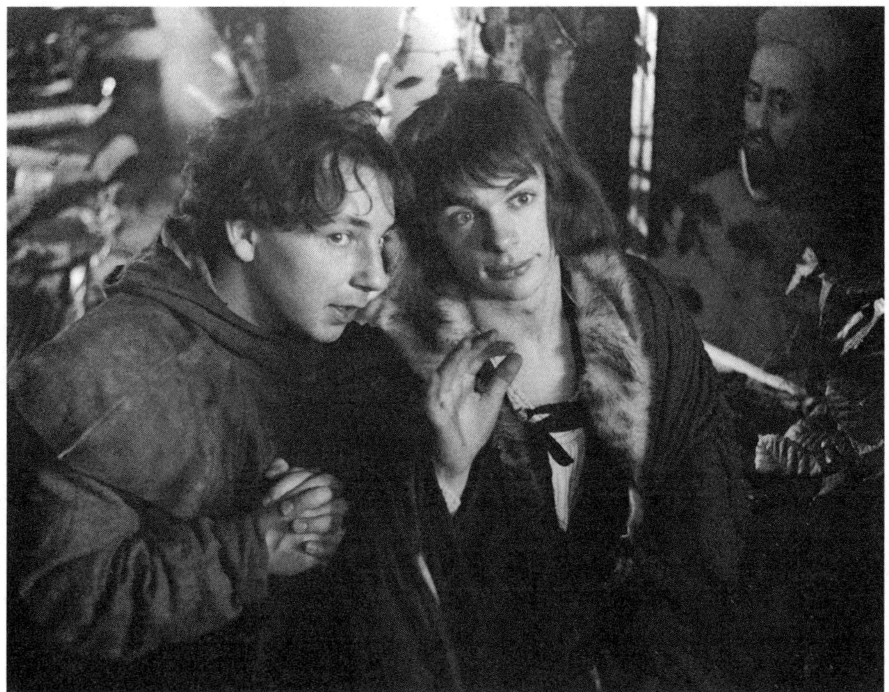

Mathias (Zbigniew Zamachowski) and Baltazar (Rafał Wieczyński) in *The Fabulous Journey of Balthazar Kober,* by W. J. Has, 1988. Copyright © Film Studio Kadr. Photo: FN. 1-F-2561-10.

Baltazar as he cleans the seminary floor. He awakens amid shards and sees his own double, who then looks down from a window at women flirting below. The parallels to *Memoirs of a Sinner* become apparent, especially because Baltazar's long hair—often under a floppy hat—adds to an androgynous appearance. Later, like Robert, he is awakened and removed from a coffin at a cemetery. (Moreover, the limping servant of Zimmermann has flowing orange hair reminiscent of Robert.)

On the one hand, Baltazar is less compelling than the hero of *Memoirs of a Sinner*, who undergoes a dramatic process of self-discovery thanks to a murderous double. On the other hand, Has's final film pairs the young protagonist with a redemptive mentor—a new variation on the theme of a young hero on a journey. Named Cammerschulze in the novel, the master represents a blend of faith, lucidity, freedom, and sacrifice. If *Fabulous Journey* includes a critique of organized religion through images of the Inquisition as well as the cardinal who receives Baltazar in a brothel— and takes his money—it also celebrates a spirituality that inheres in the natural universe. "You will descend from the arid heights of intellectual speculation to the fertile valleys where the Creator resides in every running stream," says the master. And while quietly acknowledging the horrors of the world—including misfortunes heaped on the innocent—he claims that God is there too. The reason he embraces Baltazar is that the youth is "a disciple with heart."

In *Fabulous Journey*, even the afterlife has possibilities of theme and variations. Rather than being locked in one realm, souls can move from the underworld to Paradise. When the ghost of Baltazar's mother appears, we learn she was originally sent to hell because she drowned herself; however, because her deceased children interceded on her behalf, she ascended. Later, Baltazar journeys to hell on behalf of the seminary students. The devil does not try to hold on to them; indeed, he seems nonchalant, claiming that the seminarians are prisoners of their own immobility. Hell is depicted as an externalization of the stasis that results from people's "lack of love as well as hope," in his words. One can posit that the very mobility of Has's camera represents a transcendent life force, a narrative vigor that often counterpoints his trapped individuals. (In a *Film Comment* essay of 2015, Paul Schrader makes a useful distinction between two types of camera movement—one motivated by character, the other unmotivated, occurring "when the storyteller imposes himself on the story, when the camera calls attention to itself. . . . 'Unmotivated' simply means that the camera frame reflects the director's point of view first and the characters and narrative action second."[2] Although he does not mention Has, Schrader's perception is particularly apt for this director, as when he writes, "A moving plane of focus defines time through space."[3]) Baltazar also sees his father in the lower depths and gets the angel Gabriel to carry him to Paradise.

Gabriel is one of the recurring and enigmatic images of *Fabulous Journey*. Against a dark backdrop, he brings a dazzling white sheen to the foreground, as well as slow motion to the film's rhythm. Baltazar's young brother Gaspard is linked with this angel when he appears as a ghost with unnaturally white skin. (We first see Gaspard going under a table to speak to his brother—the camera descending with him—and thus invoking Józef in *The Hourglass Sanatorium*.) Because the child gives Baltazar a jester puppet with bells, he is also connected to the actors (Pappagello's costume is similar to that of the puppet). When the boys at the seminary are cruel to Baltazar—knocking over the bucket he uses to clean the floor and jeering at him from windows above—the glass panes shatter, as if the archangel had exerted his wings.

Even if "miraculous" acts transpire, the film's heroic alternatives to fatal dogma are in the form of three human identities—actor, printer, and humanist theologian. First, Pappagello and his troupe do not simply incarnate freedom in performance but are also hiding the printer. And besides capturing Baltazar's heart, Rosa speaks to him of liberty. Zimmermann is protected by many ordinary men and women and is later allied with the master. A guard refers to him as a dangerous sorcerer, "maybe even a Jewish Kabbalist." If we are reminded of a similar character in *The Saragossa Manuscript* (played by Adam Pawlikowski), Has said, "The Kabbalah is both a deep science and a poetical vision of the world. In the *Fabulous Journey* the action takes place in a labyrinth which belongs to the realm of the Kabbalah. Such was the case with *The Saragossa Manuscript* and *The Hourglass Sanatorium*. Life is a labyrinth, we come back to the very same places, which are no longer the same because in the meantime, we have been through other experiences, other stages in our life" (French press kit of *Fabulous Journey*). There may be personal resonances, given the recollection of his widow, Wanda, that the director's father took him to Venice as a boy; moreover, his former student Małgorzata Burzyńska-Keller recalled that Has liked to say, "Venice is the labyrinth of Satan."

Perhaps the printer—a man in the service of free thought via the dissemination of words and images—represents the filmmaker, a screen sorcerer who might indeed be considered dangerous by some authorities. Writing in the *East European Film Bulletin*, Pau Bosch Santos situates Has's adaptations in the context of censorship: "It does not seem coincidental that Has' films are set during the Inquisition (*The Saragossa Manuscript*, *The Tribulations of Balthazar Kober*), the times of religion wars and witch trials in Scotland (*Memoirs of a Sinner*), the aftermaths of the failed Polish insurrection against tsarist Russia in 1863 (*The Doll*) or WWII (*Farewells*). Indeed censors, eagerly attentive, sharp and paranoid, took it as no coincidence. As Anne Guérin-Castell (the first scholar to devote a PhD thesis to Has) explains on her website, they subjected Has' films to a censure as subtle and sneaky as were the critiques the filmmaker slid into his films."[4]

There may be a self-conscious resonance toward the end of *Fabulous Journey* when Mathias greets Baltazar upon his arrival in Venice to find Strozzi. Because the latter is an organ tuner as well as the cleric who will lead the youth to safety, Mathias elaborates on how organs are a harmonious combination of shapes and tones: as each generation introduces its own innovations, "the craft links mechanical skill and metaphysics." Is this not a generous and appropriate way to describe the chapter of Polish cinema history represented by Kieślowski and Has? As Lech Majewski recalls in the documentary *Traces*, "Has's mantra was, 'we will pass away, but what we create will stay.'"[5]

Epilogue

✦

Łódź Film School

The fall of Communism a year after *The Fabulous Journey of Balthazar Kober* did not necessarily make Has's directorial efforts easier. In fact, Wanda Has suggested to me in 2015, "It was worse after Communism, when films were about the new freedom." He had been trying to film an adaptation of Blaise Pascal's *Donkey Playing the Lyre* since 1981, from his shooting script that art director Wojciech Jaworski called "exquisite and fascinating."[1] It had initially been halted because of the imposition of martial law in Poland. Although he returned to preparing this French-Polish coproduction in the 1990s, its costliness proved one of the reasons Has was unable to realize it before his death on October 3, 2000. (While official reports cited complications from diabetes as the cause, his friend Małgorzata Burzyńska-Keller told me his death resulted from an inflammation of the large intestine.) He was once again collaborating with Paris-based producer Koukou Chanska, who had coproduced his last two features. According to Ewa Mazierska and Michael Goddard, the planned cast included Orson Welles, Bette Davis, Catherine Deneuve, and Peter Ustinov.[2] (Some filmographies include *Donkey Playing the Lyre* as a production directed by Has in 1997, but they are incorrect.)

Instead, he devoted himself to his students and alumni of the Łódź Film School. He was first invited to teach directing there by Henryk Kluba in 1974 and later became *rektor* (corresponding to the title of dean in the United States) from 1990 to 1996. According to Wanda Has, "Had Kluba not offered him the teaching when he was unemployed and broke, he might have done illustrations . . . or killed himself." He clearly left a mark on the students of this internationally renowned film conservatory, despite often being enigmatic and taciturn. The website Film Polski (http://www.filmpolski.pl/fp/index.php?osoba=111519) lists the voluminous number of projects for which Wojciech Has was artistic supervisor (*opieka artystyczna*) or primary mentor (*opieka pedagogiczna*). With his focus on precision, professionalism, and finding one's own voice, he is credited with creating an oasis of free expression in Communist Poland. As Robert Gliński told me in June of 2014, "He defended his students ardently, especially when we had trouble with censorship. Ethically, he was fantastic." In 2011, thirteen directors who had studied with Has were interviewed in the documentary *Traces*. Piotr Trzaskalski recalled that Has "was like a convict, locked in a tower, waiting for the sentence, but trying to expand the tower of his imagination." Many of his pupils went on to make acclaimed features, including Gliński (*Sunday Pranks*; *Hi, Tereska*), Jolanta Dylewska (*Po-lin*; *Chronicle of the Warsaw Ghetto Uprising According to Marek Edelman*; *Children of the Night*), Borys Lankosz (*Reversal*), and Małgorzata Szumowska (*Elles*; *In the Name Of*). He is credited as the artistic supervisor on such films as *On, ona, oni* (*He, She, They*, a triptych of 1981—directed by Włodzimierz Szpak, Krzysztof Tchórzewski, Andrzej Mellin—each offering a different perspective on a marriage in dissolution), Janusz Kijowski's *Indeks: Życie i twórczość Józefa M.* (*Index: The Life and Creative Work of Joseph M.*, 1977), and Łukasz Karwowski's *Novembre* (a Polish-French production coscripted and shot by famed cinematographer Paweł Edelman, 1992), where Has is also credited as producer. Kijowski wrote about his own student days in the 1970s—on the occasion of Has being awarded an honorary doctorate in 2000—that "the Polish National Film School became an outhouse of the Propaganda Department" of the Communist Party. Although the deans "were doing their best to banish the rebellious spirit of the previous decade, . . . Wojciech J. Has saved the school from the invasion of totalitarian mediocrity, in the same way as he earlier saved the perception of Polish film from the accusation of aesthetic impotence in slavery to smooth propaganda."[3] Like other former students I interviewed at the Łódź Film School in June 2014, Kijowski expressed gratitude for Has's refusal to punish "their outside school sins" or attempts to tackle controversial subjects. Moreover, his legacy was one of extreme professionalism: "He demanded precision. He would despise artistic mess and improvisation on the set. He would oppose stupidity and laziness. He hated redundant blab and empty erudition. He would demand clarity of script and work."

Gliński, now a professor at the Łódź Film School himself (and former dean), called Has a tough individualist: "We loved his films for their idiosyncratic language. We were jealous of his long takes, which we tried to imitate. Now I show long takes in deep focus to my own students." With Has as their mentor, students watched prints that were not available on Polish screens, often obtained from the American Embassy. Gliński termed *Citizen Kane* "the Bible at the Łódź Film School in the

'70s"—calling the deep-focus shot of young Kane playing with his sled Rosebud in the background "part of our film grammar"—and elaborated on how Has taught "the master shot method, with long takes, originating in the films of John Ford, John Huston, and Westerns." (Hanna Hartowicz added that in order to see great foreign films in the 1980s, cinephiles fought to obtain tickets for the once-a-year "Confrontations" series held in Warsaw's Kino Skarpa.)

Szumowska recalled in 2015 that Has was "radically critical, with authentic irony. He didn't coddle students. He tested how tough we were to enter this brutal profession of directing. He hated realism—and said, 'Life is ugly . . . leave it to the documentarists'—believing that the world can't be naively and sentimentally assumed. He had a dark humor that perhaps informs my work."

Gliński and other Łódź alumni invoked the *Has-ufki*—a play on the Polish word *hasło* (password)—class exercises meant to reveal point of view. In English, the pun would be "Hasswords" or perhaps "Hassles." Classes were often held in Has's apartment, with students seated at the kitchen table, "where there were drawings for his unfinished *Donkey*," Gliński added. The image of Has offered by those who were close to him is multifaceted. It includes not only the architectural precision with which he drew his storyboards and the rigorous demands he made of students but also a love of women (he married four times) as well as delight in cooking. Andrzej Haliński recalled what Has considered his real prize upon returning from the 1973 Cannes Film Festival—an electric machine to make his own pasta.

Mariusz Grzegorzek, current dean of the Łódź Film School, was his student from 1984 until 1988 and then his assistant. "Has was a strong father, with great authority, and he loved playing this role. Nobody disagreed with him. He was an erudite Romantic, tied to literary tradition and the symbolic," he said during a 2014 interview in Łódź. "He was in the tradition of Kafka's fatalism. He and I got along well because of his romantic exaltation of death: I was an exalted child of the night with my own 'necrophile' side. As Klaus Kinski says in *Nosferatu*, 'we don't love the daylight.' " Identifying Has's legacy through films that reflect what is darkest in ourselves—"the real artistic energy"—he described Has as a legend who was far from communicative: "During a two-hour session, he would smoke two packs of cigarettes, blocking his mouth. He listened carefully, thought carefully, and said only two or three sentences—the essence. I heard actors say that Has spoke little on the set as well, and they often didn't know what to do. He was beyond verbal language." Although the screenwriting curriculum began at the school only after

Has's death, Grzegorzek said his classes were often devoted to discussion of screenplays. "In Poland, you could make either auteur films or commercial crap. Students had a horror of the mundane: we wanted to make something in our own names." (Since Łódź is pronounced "woodj" in Polish, set designer Maciej Putowski's pun on the school's name is worth noting—"HollyŁódź.")

Sławomir Kryński, head of directing at the Łódź School, shared vivid memories of the difference between a withdrawn Has in the classroom—"he said nothing, as if 'silence is golden' "—and the relaxed master in his own kitchen: "At home, he taught, especially after two or three glasses of gin and tonic. He inspired rather than educated. He believed form builds story." Kryński provided a few biographical details that might serve to illuminate the films: "Has left home at the age of fourteen and never had his own home. He rented rooms or lived with wives. His recurring dream was that he had to pack and leave." When I asked if this might be connected to his predilection for Jewish characters, he replied, "We're all Jews in a sense. He never acknowledged or denied being Jewish. His father was Austrian and, like his own father, he served in the Austrian army. It was Vienna rather than Warsaw. Has's mother was from Kraków, and he felt Krakovian."

Filmmaker Andrzej Krakowski—currently a professor of film at City College of New York—recalled his Łódź training during an interview in April of 2015: "Andrzej Munk and Has were our heroes in film school," he said. Because his father, Janusz Krakowski, was administrative head of the "Kamera" unit that oversaw Has's films, young Andrzej was able to visit the sets. He also saw the director at the annual Passover Seders in his family's home (where "Has eagerly took home packages of matzo") and received postcards from Has in Israel. Krakowski's own family was expelled from Poland in the anti-Semitic purge of 1968, and he recalled that the only film unit closed down at that time was "Kamera," whose artistic director, Jerzy Bossak, was Jewish.

Dariusz Jabłoński, currently one of Poland's leading independent producers, began his film career as second assistant director on Kieślowski's *Decalogue* before directing the brilliant Holocaust documentary *Photographer* (1998). He recalled about Has, "He was my professor and defended me when they were throwing me out. Finally, when I passed once again the initial exams in order to complete my film education—after *Decalogue*—he was the one who advanced me to the third year instead of starting from the beginning. There were two professors I valued the most in Łódź: Jerzy Bossak in documentary and Wojciech Jerzy Has in fiction."

Sławomir Grünberg, a New York–based filmmaker who took Has's film editing class in 1979–80, praised him as the most inspiring professor with whom he studied (in addition to Maria Kornatowska). During an interview in Manhattan in April of 2015, he fondly recalled some of Has's rules; for example, the professor insisted on holding for "twelve frames before a character starts to talk. It creates anticipation for the character to speak."

Whereas state subsidies under Communism enabled many young directors to make first features through the *zespół* (film unit) structure, the political system's collapse left a gaping hole in funding. Has therefore created the Indeks Foundation to assist Łódź graduates with aspects including fund-raising. While helping them practically, he never stopped encouraging them to be rigorous as well as independent. Today there is even a film school named after Has (as of 2009) in his beloved Kraków. When I visited in July of 2015, its director, Tomasz Gugała, explained why the private conservatory bears his name: "Has linked craft with a high aesthetic level. He paid a high price for being a nonconformist. He was the greatest of the Polish filmmakers, and his movies illustrate that nothing stimulates creativity like conflict and deprivation."

Early Shorts

The early shorts of Wojciech Has introduce thematic and stylistic elements that he would develop in his fiction features. Made in the late 1940s and early '50s, they are not as intriguing as his long-form work: the shorts reveal both individual talent and the limitations of state-imposed filmmaking. His initial training was both pictorial and literary: in early 1942 he worked for a Kraków bookstore doing graphic art, including illustrations for a book of fairy tales. Piotr Litka says that the ten black-and-white drawings signed "W. Has" "had been influenced by Walt Disney films, which fascinated this future director at the time."[1] He studied film directing in Kraków at the Film Workshop of the Young—which had been established in the former premises of the Nazi Propaganda Institute—before moving to Łódź. Then, as John Wakeman summarizes, "Between 1948 and 1951 he worked at the documentary film studios in Warsaw and from 1951 to 1956 at the educational film studios at Łódź, producing a succession of documentary, educational, and propaganda shorts on such as subjects as railroads, agriculture, and farm mechanization."[2]

After graduating from the Kraków Film Institute in 1946, Has spent a few years making documentaries before embarking on fiction features. Because *Birch Street* (*Ulica Brzozowa*, 1947), was codirected by Stanisław Różewicz, it is difficult to ascertain Has's contribution. The nine-minute film begins with a male voice-over narration introducing postwar Warsaw, bustling with construction and street life. But the fallen street sign for Birch Street introduces a darker part of Poland, where children play among the ruins of a destroyed city. "Little Hanna has been searching for sunlight," says the narrator as we see a little girl about to jump in a game of hopscotch. People of this neighborhood scrape by, but presumably with hope because a new building is being erected. "They will no longer have to live in caves and ruins," the voice says reassuringly. But, as will be the case in Has's more mature work, there is a disconnect between a jaunty sound track—both classical music and optimistic narration—and images of desolation. One tends to trust the pictures more than the words.

Harmony (*Harmonia*, 1948, 11 min.) is an auspicious fiction debut, a silent drama that—except for classical music—feels neorealist. (Most sources erroneously refer to it as "medium length": it is in fact a short.) Has creates audiovisual tension between the upbeat waltz we hear at the opening and the poignant picture of a poor boy gazing through a window at art objects in an antique store. The child runs when a man opens a window above the courtyard. This abusive shoemaker (whether he is the boy's father or employer is unclear) makes him return to work and then goes out. When the child looks down from the high window, the camera recedes in a lyrical movement that suggests his solitude. He sneaks back to the antique store, removing his boots and jacket before entering. For an accordion, he offers his possessions as well as a few coins, and finally a chain bearing a charm. Diegetic sound enables us to hear his practicing on this instrument. Has's tendency to interweave dreams into the narrative trajectory is visible when the boy is suddenly a street musician, playing the waltz we have heard. Children dance around him in a circle. That this is a dream becomes clear when the sound track offers a full orchestra instead of just one instrument, and the shoemaker dances with the antiquarian. Our young hero awakens to the furious man slapping him and throwing the accordion out the window into a puddle. But resilience seems to be the prime virtue of postwar Polish life: the boy picks up the broken pieces of his precious instrument and leaves, the music suggesting that he will succeed in forging a new path.

Locomotive (*Parowóz Pt 47*, 1949, 8 min.) is a straightforward celebration of the Polish workers who construct much-needed new trains in Poznań's Cegielski factory. The male voice-over introduces images of overcrowded trains and stations in 1946, establishing the necessity for improving transport, a "battle" for industrial growth. We see the creation of the Pt 47 locomotive, from conception and architectural drawings, to building of parts, to final assembly. (It's not surprising to find a close-up of sketches being drawn, given Has's own predilection for precisely illustrating his storyboards. Moreover, when the locomotive assumes final shape in the assembly hall, hearing the Polish word *montaż* [montage] suggests connections between a train being built and a film's construction.) The upbeat music accompanies mechanics who have earned the title of "Hero of Labor," men working toward a shared noble cause. As the new train triumphantly leaves the factory, the narrator wishes it a good trip. Can one imagine a more different depiction of a train from the ghostly opening of *The Hourglass Sanatorium* over twenty years later?

Similarly, *First Harvest* (*Pierwszy plon*, 1950, 9 min.) traces the communal labor that results in progress and a better life for Polish farmers. The Grodków cooperative in Kolnica—which has been named "Vigilance"—is the focus of this optimistic documentary, which begins with a high angle of tractors moving and ends with people singing after a successful harvest. The male voice-over at the beginning belongs to Głuszek, who addresses the group in the subsequent scene: he speaks of twelve tractor crews being established. The omniscient narrator takes over (voiced by Andrzej Łapicki, who would play the flirtatious cousin in Has's *Doll*), situating the action in June 1950 and extolling the virtues of collective life. The preparation for the harvest includes building a kindergarten so that mothers can work in the fields. "The harvest will be a hard-fought battle," he says, but we see how efficiently people have been organized into either tractor crews or reaper-binder crews (including a night-time plow system). Women working joyfully are visible throughout, and the narrator playfully says they get equal wages. He also mentions their efforts to maintain the land's fertility for the future. The Soviet combine that was sent to help the farmers is impressive, towering over the field, inseparable from the last line, "Collective life will get better each year." While *First Harvest* is clearly a documentary commissioned by the government—a piece of well-made Communist propaganda—one shot does suggest the lyrical style Has would later develop: the camera tracks a field at dusk as we hear a woman singing. Since Jan Zelnik is credited as codirector and cowriter, it is unclear how determinant a role Has played in this short; in any case, *First Harvest* is far from the kind of individualist and brooding features he would go on to direct.

My City (*Moje miasto*, 1950, 7 min.) is a more personal documentary about Has's native city of Kraków. From a text by Tadeusz Makarczyński, the male voice-over narration reminisces "between dream and reality" as images of the *rynek* (central square) are shown. Even the abundance of flowers is called "real as well as artificial." (In addition to archival footage of ordinary people, perhaps the street magician watched by a boy is an actor.) History is glimpsed through objects in a museum. "I decided to become a painter," says the narrator. "I dreamed of an art that would help people build a better life. . . . I was too young"—perhaps an early expression of Has's yearning for humanism, combined with a weary pessimism. Scenes from other movies suggest a bridge between fantasy and actuality, including a shot of a painter and an elderly dance professor watching a young girl perform. "What has remained is neither dream nor reality," the narration concludes. Even if Has did not write the text, *My City* feels like an honest glimpse at his creative roots.

Jan's Bird Feeder (*Karmik Jankovy*, 1952, 14 min.), on the other hand, seems like an atypically wholesome children's tale. Credited as J. W. Has, he might have been directing an assignment aimed at sensitizing children to the sanctity of animals. As in *Birch Street*, there is no dialogue; rather, the narrator (female) and the classical score create the tone. In this rural setting, little Jan runs to school but seems far more interested in the birds whose houses are in the nearby woods. He makes his own birdhouse for the chicks and steals them from their habitat. Although he is happy to have them hidden in his roof, the voice-over speaks of their imprisonment and isolation. After the children notice them missing, the female teacher speaks of how birds protect trees and must therefore be protected. Jan brings the birds back—first to the classroom, and then to nature—where all the children can visit them. The most interesting aspect of this short is Has's visual maturation: for example, a shot of Jan's kitchen is enhanced by the internal rhythms of a baby rocked and of his mother peeling potatoes; and when the teacher asks him to write on the blackboard, an intercut of Jan rubbing one foot against the other in close-up conveys his hesitation.

In 1952, he also directed *Herbalists from Stone Valley* (*Zielarze z Kamiennej Doliny*, 14 min.), a documentary celebrating the communal picking of herbal flowers. As J. W. Has, he traces the joyful process through which children learn to recognize, gather, and dry flowers that have medicinal value. A male voice-over introduces the story of a mountain village whose young students have been waiting for their prize of a new film projector. As the male teacher shows them the wondrous machine, a child's narration takes over, making the story subjective: "We learned that flowers yield herbs for medications . . . like wild roses providing vitamin C." During a class trip with their instructor, the students not only pick herbs but also learn the importance of drying them carefully. They continue gathering the flowers even during summer vacation. When their work is complete, the class goes into town to sell the dried herbs. "How will our work be evaluated," the child wonders. After the storekeeper looks at their huge bags, we hear the result: "It turns out we were good herbalists." Their reward is the purchase of a projector with money earned from their shared labor. Back in the present tense, the teacher projects a documentary about what later happens to the herbs: in a square inset, we see the factory process and then various drugstore windows filled with herbal teas and honeys. In a café, youngsters even enjoy herbal ice cream. (One assumes that Has shot the inner frame material as well.) The adult narrator concludes with praise for "natural national herbs," while Has portrays film viewing as a great gift.

Herbalists from Stone Valley and *Jan's Bird Feeder* are noteworthy for being his first collaborations with cinematographer Mieczysław Jahoda, who would shoot *The Noose* five years later. These shorts represent Has as a young chronicler of buoyant collective achievement. His next stage consisted of a few fiction features, often considered part of the "Polish school" that included Wajda, Jerzy Kawalerowicz, and Andrzej Munk.[3] But Has's work became increasingly personal, dark, and difficult to categorize. By the time he made *An Uneventful Story*, baby chicks were shown as the victims of ravenous crows. As he told Jerzy Wójcik—a gifted cinematographer who had also been dean of the Łódź Film School—in a filmed interview, moviemaking for him was "oneiric wandering," and the most important thing was "freedom of thought."[4]

Films are listed here by year of release (although some of the image captions contain the year of production).

Feature Films

1. *The Noose* (*Pętla*), 1957, 96 min.

Screenplay: Marek Hłasko and Wojciech Has
Cinematographer: Mieczysław Jahoda
Music: Tadeusz Baird
Production: Tadeusz Karwański, Iluzjon Studio
Cast:
 Gustaw Holoubek . . . . Kuba
 Aleksandra Śląska . . . . Krystyna
 Tadeusz Fijewski. . . . . Władek
 Teresa Szmigielówna. . . . . . Kuba's former girlfriend

2. *Farewells* (*Pożegnania*), 1958, 97 min.

Screenplay: Stanisław Dygat and Wojciech Has
Cinematographer: Mieczysław Jahoda
Music: Lucjan Kaszycki
Production: Wilhelm Hollender
Cast:
 Maria Wachowiak . . . . Lidka
 Tadeusz Janczar . . . . Paweł
 Gustaw Holoubek . . . . Mirek
 Zdzisław Mrożewski. . . . . . Paweł's father
 Irena Netto . . . . Quo Vadis landlady

3. *One Room Tenants*, or *Roommates* (*Wspólny pokój*), 1960, 92 min.

Screenplay: Wojciech Has
Cinematographer: Stefan Matyjaszkiewicz
Music: Lucjan Kaszycki
Production: Stanisław Zylewicz, Kamera Studio
Cast:

Mieczysław Gajda	Lucjan Salis
Gustaw Holoubek	Dziadzia
Adam Pawlikowski	Zygmunt Stukonis
Anna Łubieńska	Miss Leopard
Beata Tyszkiewicz	Teodozja
Zdzisław Maklakiewicz	law student

4. *Partings* (*Rozstanie*), 1961, 72 min.

Screenplay: Jadwiga Żylińska and Wojciech Has
Cinematographer: Stefan Matyjaszkiewicz
Music: Lucjan Kaszycki
Production: Stanisław Zylewicz, Studio Kamera
Cast:

Lidia Wysocka	Magdalena
Władysław Kowalski	Olek Nowak
Gustaw Holoubek	Oskar Rennert
Irena Netto	Wiktoria
Adam Pawlikowski	Żbik
Zbigniew Cybulski	actor

5. *Gold Dreams* (*Złoto*), 1962, 91 min.

Screenplay: Bohdan Czeszko
Cinematographer: Stefan Matyjaszkiewicz
Music: Lucjan Kaszycki
Production: Ryszard Straszewski, Studio Kamera
Cast:

Władysław Kowalski	young man
Krzysztof Chamiec	Piotr
Barbara Krafftówna	Zosia
Adam Pawlikowski	Piotr's friend
Elżbieta Czyżewska	Dorota

6. *How to Be Loved* (*Jak być kochaną*), 1963, 97 min.

Screenplay: Kazimierz Brandys and Wojciech Has
Cinematographer: Stefan Matyjaszkiewicz
Music: Lucjan Kaszycki
Production: Ludgierd Romanis, Studio Kamera
Cast:

    Barbara Krafftówna . . . . . . Felicja
    Zbigniew Cybulski . . . . . . Wiktor Rawicz
    Artur Młodnicki . . . . Tomasz
    Wieńczysław Gliński . . . . . . airplane passenger
    Kalina Jędrusik . . . . woman at café
    Wiesław Gołas . . . . German soldier

7. *The Saragossa Manuscript* (*Rękopis znaleziony w Saragossie*), 1965, 182 min.

Screenplay: Tadeusz Kwiatkowski and Wojciech Has, based on the novel by Jan Potocki
Cinematographer: Mieczysław Jahoda
Music: Krzysztof Penderecki
Production: Ryszard Straszewski, Studio Kamera
Cast:

    Zbigniew Cybulski . . . . . . Alfons van Worden
    Iga Cembrzyńska . . . . Emina
    Joanna Jędryka . . . . Zibelda
    Adam Pawlikowski . . . . . Uzeda
    Gustaw Holoubek . . . . . . Velasquez
    Kazimierz Opaliński . . . . . sheik/hermit
    Sławomir Lindner . . . . . . Alfons's father
    Franciszek Pieczka . . . . . . Paszeko
    Barbara Krafftówna . . . . . Camilla de Tormez,
    Beata Tyszkiewicz . . . . . . Donna Rebecca Uzeda
    Leon Niemczyk . . . . Avadoro
    Krzysztof Litwin . . . . Don Lopez Soarez
    Bogumił Kobiela . . . . Toledo
    Elżbieta Czyżewska . . . . . Frasquetta Salero
    Zdzisław Maklakiewicz . . . . Don Roque Busqueros

8. *Codes* (*Szyfry*), 1966, 80 Min.

Screenplay: Andrzej Kijowski
Cinematographer: Mieczysław Jahoda
Music: Krzysztof Penderecki, Stanisław Radwan
Production: Ryszard Straszewski, Studio Kamera
Cast:

Jan Kreczmar	Tadeusz
Zbgniew Cybulski	Maciek
Irena Eichlerówna	Zofia
Ignacy Gogolewski	Dr. Zygmunt Gross
Irena Horecka	cousin
Barbara Krafftówna	Jadwiga

9. *The Doll* (*Lalka*), 1968, 151 min.

Screenplay: Wojciech Has, based on *The Doll*, by Bolesław Prus
Cinematographer: Stefan Matyjaszkiewicz
Music: Wojciech Kilar
Production: Ryszard Straszewski, Studio Kamera
Cast:

Mariusz Dmochowski	Stanisław Wokulski
Beata Tyszkiewicz	Izabela Łęcka
Tadeusz Fijewski	Ignacy Rzecki
Andrzej Łapicki	Kazimierz Starski
Jan Kreczmar	Tomasz Łęcki, Izabela's father
Tadeusz Kondrat	Szlangbaum
Jan Machulski	Julian Ochocki

10. *The Hourglass Sanatorium* (*Sanatorium pod klepsydrą*),1973, 119 min.

Screenplay: Wojciech Has, based on stories by Bruno Schulz
Cinematographer: Witold Sobociński
Music: Jerzy Maksymiuk
Production: Urszula Orczykowska, Silesia Studio
Cast:

Jan Nowicki	Józef
Tadeusz Kondrat	Jakub, Józef's father
Irena Orska	Józef's mother

Halina Kowalska . . . . Adela
Gustaw Holoubek . . . . Dr. Gotard
Mieczysław Voit . . . . blind conductor
Bożena Adamek . . . . Bianka
Jerzy Przybylski . . . . Mr. de V.

11. *An Uneventful Story* (*Nieciekawa historia*), 1983, 106 min.

Screenplay: Wojciech Has, based on a short story by Anton Chekhov
Cinematographer: Grzegorz Kędzierski
Music: Jerzy Maksymiuk
Production: Konstanty Lewkowicz, Studio Rondo
Cast:

Gustaw Holoubek . . . . professor
Hanna Mikuć . . . . Katarzyna
Anna Milewska . . . . Weronika
Elwira Romańczuk . . . . . . Liza
Marek Bargiełowski . . . . . . Michał
Janusz Gajos. . . . . Aleksander Gnekker

12. *Write and Fight* (*Pismak*), 1985, 113 min.

Screenplay: Władysław Terlecki, based on his novel
Cinematographer: Grzegorz Kędzierski
Music: Jerzy Maksymiuk
Production: Konstanty Lewkowicz, Studio Rondo
Cast:

Wojciech Wysocki . . . . Rafał
Gustaw Holoubek . . . . investigator
Janusz Michałowski . . . . . . prison doctor
Jan Peszek . . . . Sykstus
Zdzisław Wardejn . . . . safecracker
Gabriela Kownacka . . . . . . Maria
Hanna Mikuć . . . . Sykstus's lover

13. *Memoirs of a Sinner* (*Osobisty pamiętnik grzesznika przez niego samego spisany*), 1986, 114 min.

Screenplay: Michał Komar, based on the novel by James Hogg
Cinematographer: Grzegorz Kędzierski
Music: Jerzy Maksymiuk
Production: Konstanty Lewkowicz, Studio Rondo
Cast:

Piotr Bajor	Robert
Maciej Kozłowski	the Stranger
Janusz Michałowski	Pastor Prudencjusz, Robert's father
Hanna Stankówna	Rabina, Robert's mother
Franciszek Pieczka	Logan, Rabina's husband
Ewa Wiśniewska	Laura
Anna Dymna	Dominika
Katarzyna Figura	Cyntia
Jan Jankowski	Gustaw

14. *The Fabulous Journey of Balthazar Kober* (*Niezwykła podróż Baltazara Kobera*), 1988, 115 min.

Screenplay: Wojciech Has
Cinematographer: Grzegorz Kędzierski
Music: Zdzisław Szostak
Production: Paweł Rakowski, Jean Lefevre, Studio Rondo, La Sept (France)
Cast:

Rafał Wieczyński	Baltazar
Michael Lonsdale	Cammerschulze
Daniel Emilfork	chairman
Gabriela Kownacka	Gertruda
Adrianna Biedrzyńska	Rosa
Emmanuelle Riva	mother
Evelyne Dassas	landlady
Frédéric Leidgens	Strozzi
Zbigniew Zamachowski	Mathias

Short Films

Harmony (Harmonia), 1947, 11 min.

Birch Street (Ulica Brzozowa), 1947, 9 min.
(codirected by Stanisław Różewicz)

Steam Engine (Parowóz PT 47), 1949, 8 min.

First Harvest (Pierwszy plon), 1950, 9 min.
(codirected by Jan Zelnik)

My City (Moje miasto), 1950, 7 min.

Jan's Bird Feeder (Karmik Jankovy), 1952, 14 min.
(credited as J. W. Has)

*Herbalists from Stone Valley
(Zielarze z Kamiennej Doliny)*, 1952, 14 min.

NOTES

Introduction

1. Maria Kornatowksa, "'. . . Yet We Do Not Know What Will Become of Us': On the Artistic Output of Wojciech Jerzy Has," trans. Witold Liwarowski and Richard Wawro. In *Bulletin de la Société des Sciences et des Lettres de Łódź XLV* (Series: Recherches sur les arts, Volume VI: "Polish Cinema in Ten Takes"), ed. Ewelina Nurczynska-Fidelska and Zbigniew Batko (Łódź: Łódźkie Towarzystwo Naukowe, 1995): 47.

2. Ibid., 47.

3. Michael Brooke, "The Wild Bunch: Curtain Raisers," *Sight and Sound* 19, no. 9 (September 2009): 28.

4. Marek Haltof, *Historical Dictionary of Polish Cinema* (Plymouth, U.K.: Scarecrow Press, 2007), 62.

5. Robert Kardzis, ed., *Has: Unattainable* (Wrocław: MFF Nowe Horyzonty/ Era New Horizons, 2010), 32.

6. Ewa Mazierska, "Wojciech Jerzy Has at Era New Horizons International Film Festival, Wrocław, Poland, 22 July–1 August 2010," *Studies in Eastern European Cinema* 2, no. 1 (March 2011): 123–25.

7. Ado Kyrou, *Le surréalisme au cinéma* (Paris: Terrain Vague, 1985), 151.

8. Luis Buñuel, *My Last Sigh* (New York: Vintage Books, 1984), 224. According to Has's obituary in the *Los Angeles Times*, when *How to Be Loved* received the grand prize at the San Francisco Film Festival in 1963, it was "bestowed by Luis Buñuel, who borrowed elements from *Saragossa* for his own 1967 *Belle du Jour* and subsequent masterpieces" (Myrna Oliver, "Wojciech Has; Directed Polish Film Masterpiece," *Los Angeles Times*, October 6, 2000, http://articles. latimes.com/2000/oct/06/local/me-32227).

9. Paul Cronin, ed., *Roman Polanski: Interviews* (Jackson: University Press of Mississippi, 2005), 6: "Among Polish talents who are unknown here in France is Wojciech Has who made a film called *The Art of Loving*." The correct title translation is *How to Be Loved*.

Chapter 1

1. Kieślowski will use the same composition in *Decalogue, 9*: a telephone in the left foreground visually overpowers the impotent doctor Roman.

2. Fijewski began acting in film and theater at the age of ten, before and after World War II—during which he was in a concentration camp as well as part of the Warsaw Uprising. Has worked with him again in *Gold Dreams* and in *The Doll*.

3. Marek Haltof, *Polish National Cinema* (New York: Berghahn Books, 2002), 81.

4. Roger Ebert, "*Leaving Las Vegas*," Rogerebert.com, April 25, 2004, http:// www.rogerebert.com/reviews/great-movie-leaving-las-vegas-1995.

5. Ewa Nawój and Agnieszka Le Nart, "Wojciech Jerzy Has," Culture.pl, April 2011, http://culture.pl/en/artist/wojciech-jerzy-has.

6. Bartosz Staszczyszyn, translated with edits by Paulina Schlosser, May 2, 2014; translations of Hłasko and author quotes by Paulina Schlosser; http://culture.pl/en/article/artists-in-the-land-of-wodka.

7. Nick Roddick, "Wojciech Has: Curiouser and Curiouser," British Film Institute, *Sight and Sound*, February 7, 2014, http://www.bfi.org.uk/news-opinion/sight-sound-magazine/features/wojciech-has-curiouser-curiouser.

Chapter 2

1. Lidka's fondness is most likely for the 1951 Hollywood film version, based on Henryk Sienkiewicz's novel of 1896. The Polish film adaptation by Jerzy Kawalerowicz would appear only in 2001.

2. Anna M. Zarychta and Piotr Litka, eds., *Pamiętasz, była jesień: Wspomnienia o Wojciechu Jerzym Hasie* (Łódź: Wydawnictwo PWSFTviT, 2010), 38.

3. The song lyrics, from an online source (http://lyricstranslate.com/en/pamietasz-byla-jesien-do-you-remember-it-was-fall.html) are as follows:

> Do you remember, it was autumn,
> The small hotel Under the Roses, room number 8.
> An elderly porter, smiling, gave us the key.
> On the stairs, impatiently,
> You furtively kissed my hair.
> Whether there were more golden leaves then
> Than your caresses, dear,
> Today I no longer know.
> Then you left suddenly, the door ajar,
> A windblown leaf fell at my feet
> And then I understood: here it ends.
> It's time to cross the threshold of parting.
>
> Do you remember, it was autumn,
> Room number 8, the foggy hallway.
> I will never forget the small hotel Under the Roses
> Although a year has passed.
> My love, return to me, I long for you.
> Don't let partings, beloved, ever separate us again.
> Stop the trains, and may the postman never again
> Deliver bad letters to the hotel of roses.

4. A symposium held in May 1999 in Poznań led to a special issue of *Music and Film*. It includes an essay by Julia Michałowska that considers "*Pamiętasz, była jesień*" as a source text for the movie, attributing "a song-like construction of stanzas-and-refrain" to its shape (Julia Michałowska, "*Chanson Triste*—About *Pożegnania* [Farewells] by Wojciech Jerzy Has," *Music and Film* [published in Poznań], 2002, 117–22).

Chapter 3

1. Zarychta and Litka, *Pamiętasz, była jesień*, 41. Beata Tyszkiewicz recalled that *One Room Tenants* was the first of three collaborations with Has and

likened the early film to a "chamber piece": unlike the bigger budgeted *Saragossa Manuscript* and *The Doll*, it was "an ascetic shoot, with no money for multiple takes."

2. Ibid., 16.

3. Haltof, *Polish National Cinema*, 82.

4. Ewa Mazierska, "Existentialism and Socialist Realism in the Early Films of Wojciech Has," *Studies in Eastern European Cinema* 4, no. 1 (January 2013): 19.

5. Kardzis, *Has: Unattainable*, 66.

Chapter 4

1. Zarychta and Litka, eds., *Pamiętasz, była jesień*, 46. *Partings* was Władysław Kowalski's first film after starring in a Polish stage version of *A Taste of Honey*. He recalled being the youngest and least experienced cast member; the director had to spend more time with him, but "Has had a voracious embrace for those he really liked."

2. Ibid., 14.

3. Ibid., 30. Composer Lucjan Kaszycki was distraught when he saw the final film and realized the song would merely accompany the opening credits: "The windshield wipers of the truck destroyed the tune," he claimed.

4. Bolesław Michałek and Frank Turaj, *The Modern Cinema of Poland* (Bloomington: Indiana University Press, 1988), 33.

Chapter 5

1. Mazierska, "Existentialism and Socialist Realism," 25.

2. Krzysztof-Teodor Toeplitz, "The Films of Wojciech Has," *Film Quarterly* 18, no. 2 (Winter 1964): 6.

Chapter 6

1. That Resnais's heroine is never named in *Hiroshima, mon amour* can be juxtaposed with Żaneta Jamrozik's suggestion that "'Felicja' could just as well be called 'the actress', as she remains unnamed both in the novel and in the film" (Żaneta Jamrozik, "How to Be an Actress [in Poland]: The Figure of the Actress in Wojciech Jerzy Has's *How to Be Loved* [1962]," *Studies in Eastern European Cinema* 4, no. 1 [January 2013]: 33).

2. Kieślowski would use a similar tracking along the line of a highway in *Decalogue, 9*.

3. There are alternative endings, including the double suicide of Odette and Siegfried; his suicide after he inadvertently kills his beloved; and the version danced by the National Ballet of Canada in 2010, in which Odette is left alone to mourn the dead Siegfried. This is the ending closest to the scenario of *How to Be Loved*.

4. A nine-minute interview with Barbara Krafftówna (without English subtitles) was filmed in Warsaw in 2008 and can be seen on YouTube: http://www.youtube.com/watch?v=oGxT7x9XP6w. The actress speaks warmly of Has as "a phenomenally sensitive artist" with a precise vision and perfectionist preparation. She acknowledges the unusually long dialogue scenes of *How to Be Loved* and their "literary weight." After recalling that she wanted to lower her gaze in one scene, "feeling that my character would do so," the actress adds Has's

response: "Okay, but we will do one take like that, and one the other way." Krafftówna makes a distinction between Brandys's screenplay (*scenariusz*) and Has's shooting script (*scenopis*), which included all the cinematic layers. "Today, after many years," she concludes, "I always analyze why the film doesn't age. Are there universal themes that transcend eras?" These depend on the "phenomenal realization" of Has.

5. While a white horse appears symbolically in *Ashes and Diamonds*, Columbia University student Justin Restivo noticed in *How to Be Loved* a striking repetition of horses, beginning with a glimpse of the carriage that takes Felicja and Wiktor to the wartime hiding place. When Wiktor approaches the bar (before he serves coffee and cognac to Peters and the Nazis), a painting of a horse is seen in the background. Later, a single horse is visible in the alley when the Soviet tanks ride into Kraków. After the committee bars Felicja from performing, she feeds a horse before entering the adjoining carriage. And when Tomasz visits her in Warsaw, one of the production assistants gives him a tip about a horse race. (Felicja comments on his faith in a single horse.) If the horse has functioned as a symbol of Poland's national identity (similar to the military regalia in *Ashes and Diamonds*), a different Shakespeare play comes to mind: in *Richard III*, the famous line is "My kingdom for a horse." Don't many of these films examine the postwar winter of Poland's discontent?

6. Stowarzyszenie Willa Decjusza, "Kazimierz Brandys," Culture.pl, 2001, http://culture.pl/en/artist/kazimierz-brandys.

7. Ibid.

8. Eugenia Prokop-Janiec, "Brandys, Kazimierz," trans. Christina Manetti, in *The YIVO Encyclopedia of Jews in Eastern Europe*, http://www.yivoencyclopedia .org/article.aspx/Brandys_Kazimierz.

9. Jamrozik, "How to Be an Actress," 30.

Chapter 7

1. Garcia died in 1995 at the age of fifty-three, before being able to enjoy viewing the film again in Berkeley. *The Saragossa Manuscript* DVD that was released by Image Entertainment in 2008 contains superbly comprehensive liner notes by Darren Gross and Nathaniel Thompson. They trace the investigative work involved in the restoration, mentioning that Garcia died the day before the print was inspected. It turned out that Has had the only remaining print of the complete version.

2. In his *Village Voice* review of April 1, 2008, J. Hoberman explained that "*The Saragossa Manuscript* first blew minds at the 1966 San Francisco Film Festival, attracting a New York hippie following six years later with a midnight run at the old Elgin theater. At some point, Jerry Garcia signed on as the movie's biggest booster, donating a print to the Pacific Film Archives on the condition that he'd always be able to screen it."

3. For a more extensive plot summary, see the liner notes of Darren Gross and Nathaniel Thompson that accompany the Image Entertainment DVD.

4. Peter Keough, "Cinema Lacking Polish?" *Boston Phoenix*, August 7, 2009, http://blog.thephoenix.com/BLOGS/outsidetheframe/archive/2009/08/07/ cinema-lacking-polish.aspx.

5. Darragh O'Donoghue, "*The Saragossa Manuscript*," *Senses of Cinema*, no. 64 (August 2012), http://sensesofcinema.com/2012/cteq/the-saragossa-manuscript/.

6. Izabela Kalinowska, "From Orientalism to Surrealism: Wojciech Jerzy Has Interprets Jan Potocki," *Studies in Eastern European Cinema* 4, no. 1 (January 2013): 48.

7. Ibid., 59.

8. Jan Potocki, *The Manuscript Found in Saragossa*, trans. Ian Maclean (London: Penguin, 1996), 3.

9. Phillip Lopate, Report on New York Film Festival, *Film Comment* 33, no. 6 (November–December 1997): 64.

10. Potocki, *Manuscript Found in Saragossa*, 630.

11. Kalinowska, "From Orientalism to Surrealism," 60.

12. Ibid., 57. Kalinowska writes, "Potocki's Orientalism in *The Manuscript* is not meant to provide a rationale for European imperialism. Quite the contrary, he speaks against cultural Eurocentrism. His voice is—not unlike that of the surrealists a century later—anarchic and anti-hierarchical. He brings all of the marginalized peoples of modern Europe into centre stage, and reaches outside of Europe, towards the Muslim Orient, to argue that all cultures are equal, and exist in dialogue with other cultures, as their development is part of the historical process."

13. A half-hour documentary about the making of *The Saragossa Manuscript* was directed by Ryszard Bugajski for the Polish television station TVP in 1998. Containing interviews with many cast and crew members, "Filmy o filmach, czyli jak powstawała Saragossa (Wojciech Jerzy Has)" can be found on YouTube (but without English subtitles) at https://www.youtube.com/watch?v=osSi7GJqrcU.

Cinematographer Mieczysław Jahoda recalls that CinemaScope was a necessity for this story: "Today it would have been made in color," he added. "But there wasn't enough color stock at the time." Production and costume designer Jerzy Skarżyński says that he and his wife, Lidia, designed all the costumes in a palette of black, white, and gray.

Barbara Pec-Ślesicka, production manager, specifies that they had seven months of preparation. A few people interviewed talk about Zbigniew Cybulski being the third choice to play Alfons. The shoot began with André Cler, who claimed he was a French actor. After a few days on set, he was fired; moreover, he turned out to be Polish and a liar. Has wanted to replace him with an actor named Zbigniew Wójcik, but he committed suicide.

The history of André Cler's participation was confirmed by City College film professor Andrzej Krakowski when he introduced *The Saragossa Manuscript* at a Brooklyn Academy of Music retrospective of Has's work on October 17, 2015. He added that the film was "a tough sell to Polish authorities—an eighteenth-century book, by an aristocrat (the regime hated those), and in French, having nothing to do with Poland."

Chapter 8

1. Małgorzata Jakubowska, Kamila Żyto, Anna M. Zarychta, eds. *Filmowe ogrody* (Cinematic Gardens) *Wojciecha Jerzego Hasa* (Łódź: Wydawnictwo PWFSFTviT, 2011).

2. Similar themes inform *Ida*, Paweł Pawlikowski's acclaimed film of 2013, whose focus is a young woman about to become a nun in the Poland of 1962.

When her aunt Wanda helps Ida investigate her Jewish roots, the film centers on the questions, what happened to my son during the war? Was he killed, and—if so—by Nazis or Poles? However, the grip of the past is implied rather than shown in flashbacks.

3. This might be one of the film's gentle digs at Communism and its disapproval of "Western music." Moreover, when Dr. Gross offers Tadeusz a drink, he apologizes that the liquor is Russian. This eye-winking acknowledgment of Communist control is crystallized when Tadeusz asks the man in the bookstore, "Are you the owner?" He answers, "I'm the manager; the owner is the working class." Moreover, Kijowski (1928–85) was a leading Polish writer and opponent of Communism. In the early 1970s, he traveled to the United States, invited by the University of Iowa International Writing Program.

Chapter 9

1. Haltof, *Polish National Cinema*, 116.

2. Elżbieta Ostrowska, "Dreaming, Drifting, Dying: The Narrative Inertia in Wojciech Has's *Lalka/The Doll* (1968)," *Studies in Eastern European Cinema* 4, no. 1 (January 2013): 66.

3. Paul Coates, "'Choose the Impossible': Wojciech Has Reframes Prus's *Lalka*," *Studies in Eastern European Cinema* 4, no. 1 (January 2013): 79.

4. Ostrowska, "Dreaming, Drifting, Dying," makes a connection between the immobilized human figure of Has's film and the issue of social immobility (69), particularly because we never see the hero's travels: "The narrative convinces us of his mobility, yet it does not translate into an actual on-screen physical movement" (71).

5. There was also a Polish TV miniseries of *The Doll* in 1977, directed by Ryszard Ber. The combination of formats reflects that Prus's novel was published in two ways: like the work of Charles Dickens, it was serialized between 1887 and 1889 before appearing as a novel in 1889. A musical version of *The Doll* was presented in Gdynia in 2010, directed by Wojciech Kościelniak, and broadcast on Polish television a year later. Some of the actors moved and acted like puppets.

6. Ostrowska, "Dreaming, Drifting, Dying," 76.

Chapter 10

1. Steve Mobia, "The Sandglass: A Journey into the Underworld," 1983, http://stevemobia.com/WriteSubPages/journey.htm.

2. The English subtitles of an early version curiously mistranslated the Polish dialogue by adding a Christian context, "lined up like rosary beads."

3. Bruno Schulz, *Sanatorium under the Sign of the Hourglass*, trans. Celina Wieniewska (New York: Penguin Books, 1979), 131. Schulz's own drawings in the Penguin edition are fascinating complements to his tales. Etched onto spoiled photographic plates that he obtained from drugstores, they are signs of a feverish imagination.

4. Ibid., xii.

5. Ibid., xvii.

6. Ibid., 38.

7. Ibid., 61.

8. Ibid., 113.

9. Ibid., 117.

10. https://www.youtube.com/watch?v=SxtBYCm3oxc.

11. Adam Garbicz, Review of *The Hourglass* (*Sanatorium pod klepsydrą*), by Wojciech Has, *Film Quarterly* 28, no. 3 (Spring 1975): 62.

12. Ibid., 62.

13. David Melville, "'The Fiery Beauty of the World': Wojciech Has and *The Hourglass Sanatorium*," *Senses of Cinema*, no. 64 (August 2012), http://sensesofcinema.com/2012/cteq/the-fiery-beauty-of-the-world-wojciech-has-and-the-hourglass-sanatorium/.

14. *Żydzi polscy: Historie niezwykłe* (Polish Jews: Unusual Tales) (Warsaw: Demart, 2010), 113.

15. Nick Hodge, "Wojciech Has and the Interpretation of Dreams," *Krakow Post*, August 7, 2010, http://www.krakowpost.com/2265/2010/08.

Chapter 11

1. During a June 2015 interview in Warsaw, Kędzierski acknowledged the extent to which birds constitute a motif in *An Uneventful Story*: "I shot Katia's face to find a resemblance to birds—for example, in the tense head movements. When she appears in the last scene, there is a bird in her hat too. Has deleted interesting shots, like a bird knocking against the professor's window. He had a sharp sense of what was essential, treating the viewer as a partner toward mutual understanding."

2. "There have been a few legends about Has's exceptionally precise shooting scripts," Kędzierski wrote. "The fact is that he was always perfectly prepared for working on set and never tolerated chaos. . . . Has's shooting scripts, which included all his artistic work together with the setting and visual design, and many other indications of his in-depth intellectual preparation, constituted only one of the many stages of this director's unique creative method" (Kardzis, *Nowe Horyzonty/Era*, 154).

3. Anton Chekhov, "A Boring Story," in *Selected Stories of Anton Chekhov*, trans. Richard Pevear and Larissa Volokhonsky, 55–107 (New York: Modern Library, 2000).

4. Alicja Helman, "The Masters Are Tired," *Canadian Slavonic Papers* 42, no. 1/2 (March–June 2000): 102.

5. PaczeMoj, "*An Uneventful Story*," FilmJerk.com, May 7, 2007, http://www.filmjerk.com/reviews/article.php?id_rev=1127.

Chapter 12

1. Kardzis, *Nowe Horyzonty/Era*, 160.

2. Kędzierski recalled in our 2015 interview that this scene initially came out "too realistic" and had to be done over: "Has never shot in natural exteriors. This particular décor was in four of his films. Even the firing squad scene of *Write and Fight* was redone because the sun was shining in the first version, too sugar-coated. The shooting ratio was 4:1, with tracking master shots of ten minutes that were then edited."

Chapter 13

1. David Cairns, "The Forgotten: Both of Me," MUBI, November 14, 2013, https://mubi.com/notebook/posts/the-forgotten-both-of-me.

2. Ibid.

3. Melville, "Fiery Beauty of the World," 3.

4. Anne Guérin-Castell, "Wojciech Has, un cinéaste libre (1): Le pouvoir," Medi-apart, June 11, 2008, https://blogs.mediapart.fr/blog/anne-guerin-castell/110608/wojciech-has-un-cineaste-libre-1-le-pouvoir.

5. Helman, "The Masters Are Tired," 101.

Chapter 14

1. Rafał Wieczyński recalled that he was offered the lead role in Kieślowski's *Short Film About Love* at the same time as Has's film: "In the end, Olaf Lubaszenko got the part, and I chose *Kober*" (Kardzis, *Nowe Horyzonty/Era*, 178).

2. Paul Schrader, "Game Changers: Camera Movement," *Film Comment* 51, no. 2 (March/April 2015): 57.

3. Ibid., 58.

4. Pau Bosch Santos, "Wojciech Has: The Silent Rebel," *East European Film Bulletin*, October 14, 2014, http://eefb.org/archive/october-2014/wojciech-has-the-silent-rebel/.

5. *Traces* (*Ślady*), directed by Robert Gliński (Łódź: Studio Filmowe Indeks, PWSFTviT, 2012), film, 53 min.

Epilogue

1. Kardzis, *Nowe Horyzonty/Era*, 186.

2. Ewa Mazierska and Michael Goddard, "The Unjustly Neglected Career of Wojciech Jerzy Has," *Studies in Eastern European Cinema* 4, no. 1 (January 2013): 5.

3. Janusz Kijowski, "The Artist in School," in *Doktor Honoris Causa*, 1–8 (Łódź, 2000).

Appendix: Early Shorts

1. Kardzis, *Nowe Horyzonty/Era*, 16.

2. John Wakeman, ed., *World Film Directors: Volume Two, 1945–1985* (New York: Wilson, 1988), 414.

3. The Polish school has been defined as a movement from 1956 to 1962, comprising three elements: "First, a canon of critical realism appeared determined to present life as it truly was in Poland's society. Second, films were made about recent history, the war, occupation, the immediate postwar period. . . . Third, a number of filmmakers turned away from socialist realism so far as to concentrate on psychological as well as literary quality . . ." (Michałek and Turaj, *Modern Cinema of Poland*, 21).

4. "Utwór filmowy: Spotkanie z Wojciechem Hasem," YouTube, video, 14 min., https://www.youtube.com/watch?v=ZZfNgxekEVY. The film features Jerzy Wójcik interviewing Has and includes clips from *Codes*.

Brooke, Michael. "Wojciech Has" in "The Wild Bunch: Curtain Raisers," ed. Mark Cousins. *Sight and Sound* 19, no. 9 (September 2009): 22–36.

Buñuel, Luis. *My Last Sigh*. New York: Vintage Books, 1984.

Cairns, David. "The Forgotten: Both of Me." MUBI, November 14, 2013. https://mubi.com/notebook/posts/the-forgotten-both-of-me.

Chekhov, Anton. "A Boring Story." In *Selected Stories of Anton Chekhov*, translated by Richard Pevear and Larissa Volokhonsky, 55–107. New York: Modern Library, 2000.

Coates, Paul. "'Choose the Impossible': Wojciech Has Reframes Prus's *Lalka*." *Studies in Eastern European Cinema* 4, no. 1 (January 2013): 79–94.

Eberhardt, Konrad. *Wojciech Has*. Warsaw: Wydawnictwa Artystyczne i Filmowe, 1967.

Ebert, Roger. "*Leaving Las Vegas*." Rogerebert.com, April 25, 2004. http://www.rogerebert.com/reviews/great-movie-leaving-las-vegas-1995.

Fuksiewicz, Jacek. *Le cinéma polonais*. Paris: Cerf, 1989.

Garbicz, Adam. Review of *The Hourglass* (*Sanatorium pod klepsydrą*), by Wojciech Has. *Film Quarterly* 28, no. 3 (Spring 1975): 59–62.

Grodź, Iwona. *Zaszyfrowane w obrazie: O filmach Wojciecha Jerzego Hasa* (Encrypted in the Image: On the Films of Wojciech Jerzy Has). Gdańsk: Słowo/Obraz Terytoria, 2008.

Guérin-Castell, Anne. "Wojciech Has, un cinéaste libre (1): Le pouvoir." Mediapart, June 11, 2008. https://blogs.mediapart.fr/anne-guerin-castell/blog/110608/wojciech-has-un-cineaste-libre-1-le-pouvoir.

Haltof, Marek. *Historical Dictionary of Polish Cinema*. Plymouth, U.K.: Scarecrow Press, 2007.

———. *Polish National Cinema*. New York: Berghahn Books, 2002.

Has, Jadwiga. *Życie w drugim planie* (Life in the Background). Warsaw: Skorpion, 2010.

Helman, Alicja. "The Masters Are Tired." *Canadian Slavonic Papers* 42, no. 1/2 (March–June 2000): 99–111.

Hoberman, J. Review of *The Saragossa Manuscript*. *Village Voice*, April 1, 2008.

Hodge, Nick. "Wojciech Has and the Interpretation of Dreams." *Krakow Post*, August 7, 2010. http://www.krakowpost.com/2265/2010/08.

"Jak być kochaną, Barbara Krafftówna, Warszawa 2008." YouTube, video, 9:42. https://www.youtube.com/watch?v=oGxT7x9XP6w.

Jakubowska, Małgorzata. *Kryształy czasu: Kino Wojciecha Jerzego Hasa* (Crystals of Time: The Cinema of Wojciech Jerzy Has). Łódź: Wydawnictwo PWSFTviT, 2013.

———. *Laboratorium czasu* (Laboratory of Time): *"Sanatorium pod klepsydrą" Wojciecha Jerzego Hasa*. Łódź: Wydawnictwo PWSFTviT, 2010.

Jakubowska, Małgorzata, Kamila Żyto, and Anna M. Zarychta, eds. *Filmowe ogrody Wojciecha Jerzego Hasa* (Łódź: Wydawnictwo PWFSFTviT, 2011).

Jamrozik, Żaneta. "How to Be an Actress (in Poland): The Figure of the Actress in Wojciech Jerzy Has's *How to Be Loved* (1962)." *Studies in Eastern European Cinema* 4, no. 1 (January 2013): 29–46.

Kalinowska, Izabela. "From Orientalism to Surrealism: Wojciech Jerzy Has Interprets Jan Potocki." *Studies in Eastern European Cinema* 4, no. 1 (January 2013): 47–62.

Kardzis, Robert, ed. *Has: Unattainable*. MFF Nowe Horyzonty, Wrocław, 2010.

Keough, Peter. "Cinema Lacking Polish?" *Boston Phoenix*, August 7, 2009. http://blog.thephoenix.com/BLOGS/outsidetheframe/archive/2009/08/07/cinema-lacking-polish.aspx.

Kijowski, Janusz. "The Artist in School." In *Doktor Honoris Causa*, 1–8. Łódź, 2000.

Kornatowksa, Maria. "'. . . Yet We Do Not Know What Will Become of Us': On the Artistic Output of Wojciech Jerzy Has." Translated by Witold Liwarowski and Richard Wawro. In *Bulletin de la Société des Sciences et des Lettres de Lodz XLV* (Series: Recherches sur les arts, Volume VI: "Polish Cinema in Ten Takes"), ed. Ewelina Nurczynska-Fidelska and Zbigniew Batko (Łódź: Łódźkie Towarzystwo Naukowe, 1995), 39–49.

Kyrou, Ado. *Le surréalisme au cinéma*. Paris: Terrain Vague, 1985.

Lopate, Phillip. Report on New York Film Festival. *Film Comment* 33, no. 6 (November–December 1997): 60–65.

Maron, Marcin. *Dramat czasu i wyobraźni* (The Drama of Time and Imagination): *Filmy Wojciecha J. Hasa*. Kraków: Towarzystwo Autorów i Wydawców Prac Naukowych "Universitas," 2010.

Mazierska, Ewa. "Existentialism and Socialist Realism in the Early Films of Wojciech Has." *Studies in Eastern European Cinema* 4, no. 1 (January 2013): 9–27.

———. "Wojciech Jerzy Has at Era New Horizons International Film Festival, Wrocław, Poland, 22 July–1 August 2010." *Studies in Eastern European Cinema* 2, no. 1 (March 2011): 123–25.

Mazierska, Ewa, and Michael Goddard. "The Unjustly Neglected Career of Wojciech Jerzy Has." *Studies in Eastern European Cinema* 4, no. 1 (January 2013): 3–7.

Melville, David. "'The Fiery Beauty of the World': Wojciech Has and *The Hourglass Sanatorium*." *Senses of Cinema*, no. 64 (August 2012). http://sensesofcinema.com/2012/cteq/the-fiery-beauty-of-the-world-wojciech-has-and-the-hourglass-sanatorium/.

Michałek, Bolesław, and Frank Turaj. *The Modern Cinema of Poland*. Bloomington: Indiana University Press, 1988.

Michałowska, Julia. "*Chanson Triste*—About *Pożegnania* (Farewells) by Wojciech Jerzy Has." *Music and Film* (Poznań), 2002, 117–22.

Mobia, Steve. "The Sandglass: A Journey into the Underworld," 1983. http://stevemobia.com/WriteSubPages/journey.htm.

Nawój, Ewa, and Agnieszka Le Nart. "Wojciech Jerzy Has." Culture.pl, April 2011. http://culture.pl/en/artist/wojciech-jerzy-has.

O'Donoghue, Darragh. "*The Saragossa Manuscript.*" *Senses of Cinema*, no. 64 (August 2012). http://sensesofcinema.com/2012/cteq/the-saragossa-manuscript/.

Oliver, Myrna. "Wojciech Has; Directed Polish Film Masterpiece." *Los Angeles Times*, October 6, 2000. http://articles.latimes.com/2000/oct/06/local/me -32227.

Ostrowska, Elżbieta. "Dreaming, Drifting, Dying: The Narrative Inertia in Wojciech Has's *Lalka/The Doll* (1968)." *Studies in Eastern European Cinema* 4, no. 1 (January 2013): 63–78.

Out of a Dream, a Dream. Directed by Adam Kuczyński, Polish Television (Warsaw), 1998. Film, 40 min.

PaczeMoj. "*An Uneventful Story.*" FilmJerk.com, May 7, 2007. http://www.film jerk.com/reviews/article.php?id_rev=1127.

Potocki, Jan. *The Manuscript Found in Saragossa.* Translated by Ian Maclean. London: Penguin, 1996.

Prokop-Janiec, Eugenia. "Brandys, Kazimierz." Translated by Christina Manetti. In *The YIVO Encyclopedia of Jews in Eastern Europe.* 2010. http://www.yivo encyclopedia.org/article.aspx/Brandys_Kazimierz.

Roddick, Nick. "Wojciech Has: Curiouser and Curiouser." British Film Institute. *Sight and Sound*, February 7, 2014. http://www.bfi.org.uk/news-opinion/ sight-sound-magazine/features/wojciech-has-curiouser-curiouser.

Santos, Pau Bosch. "Wojciech Has: The Silent Rebel." *East European Film Bulletin*, October 14, 2014. http://eefb.org/archive/october-2014/wojciech-has-the -silent-rebel/.

Schrader, Paul. "Game Changers: Camera Movement." *Film Comment* 51, no. 2 (March/April 2015). http://www.filmcomment.com/article/game-changers -camera-movement/.

Schulz, Bruno. *Sanatorium under the Sign of the Hourglass.* Translated by Celina Wieniewska. New York: Penguin Books, 1979.

Stowarzyszenie Willa Decjusza. "Kazimierz Brandys." Culture.pl, 2001. http:// culture.pl/en/artist/kazimierz-brandys.

Toeplitz, Krzysztof-Teodor. "The Films of Wojciech Has." *Film Quarterly* 18, no. 2 (Winter 1964): 2–6.

Traces (Ślady). Directed by Robert Gliński. Łódź: Studio Filmowe Inde ks, PWS-FTviT, 2012. Film, 53 min.

Zarychta, Anna M., and Piotr Litka, eds. *Pamiętasz, była jesień: Wspomnienia o Wojciechu Jerzym Hasie* (Remember, It Was Autumn: Memories of Wojciech Jerzy Has). Łódź: Wydawnictwo PWSFTviT, 2010.

"Utwór filmowy: Spotkanie z Wojciechem Hasem" (Film Work: Meeting with Wojciech Has). YouTube, video, 14 min. https://www.youtube.com/ watch?v=ZZfNgxekEVY.

Żydzi polscy: Historie niezwykłe (Polish Jews: Unusual Tales). Warsaw: Demart, 2010.

INDEX

Page numbers in *italic* indicate photographs; **bold** page numbers indicate filmography.

"About the Evening Guest," 28–29
Adam Mickiewicz Institute (Warsaw), 3, 45
alcoholism, 12–14, 33
Anderson, Lindsay, 101
anti-Semitism, 21, 58–59, 68, 80, 112
Antonioni, Michelangelo, 36
Arakcheyev, Aleksey, 86
Ashes and Diamonds (1958), 11, 17–19, 36–37, 43–44, 55–56
Auschwitz, 17, 33, 35, 58, 59

Baird, Tadeusz, and *The Noose* (1957), 11
Bajor, Piotr, in *Memoirs of a Sinner* (1986), 97, *101*
Barbican (London), 13–14
Basehart, Richard, 36
Beckett, Samuel, 44, 81
Beethoven, Ludwig van, 49
Bergman, Ingmar, 61
Bergman, Ingrid, 82
Bergt, Siena, 9
Biedrzyńska, Adrianna, in *The Fabulous Journey of Balthazar Kober* (1988), 104
Birch Street (*Ulica Brzozowa*, 1947), 115, 118, **127**
Blind Chance (1987), 3–4
Bogarde, Dirk, 21
Bosch Santos, Pau, 107
Bossak, Jerzy, 112
Boston Phoenix, 51–52
Brandys, Kazimierz, 79; and *The Doll* (1968), 65; and *How to Be Loved* (1963), 39, 44–45, 65
Brooke, Michael, 4–5
Brooklyn Academy of Music, 47
Buñuel, Luis, 6, 47, 129n8
Burzyńska-Keller, Małgorzata, 5, 80–81, 107, 109

Cage, Nicolas, 12
Cairns, David, 100, 101

Camus, Albert, 44
Cannes Film Festival, 44, 82, 87–88, 111
Carrière, Jean-Claude, 47
censorship, 4, 95, 107, 110
Chamiec, Krzysztof, in *Gold Dreams* (1962), 33
Chanska, Koukou, 109
Chekhov, Anton, 31, 65, 70, 83, 86–87
Chopin, Frédéric, 18
Citizen Kane (1941), 100, 110–11
City College of New York, 112
Clark, Chantel, 77
Cmentarze, 12
Coates, Paul, 67
Codes (*Szyfry*, 1966), 57–63, 77, **124**; comparison with other films, 61, 63; music and sound design, 62–63
Columbia University, 3, 9, 10–11, 77
Communism/Communist Party, 4, 13–14, 15, 44–45, 59, 80, 87–88, 109–11, 113, 117, 134n3 (chap. 8)
Coppola, Francis Ford, 47
Cybulski, Zbigniew, 18; and *Codes* (1966), 57, *62*; in *How to Be Loved* (1963), 39, 43; in *The Saragossa Manuscript* (1965), 48, 49, 51, 133n13
Czekalski, Andrzej: and *Farewells* (1958), 19, 24; and *One Room Tenants* (1960), 24
"Czerwone maki na Monte Cassino" ("The Red Poppies on Monte Cassino"), 43
Czeszko, Bohdan, and *Gold Dreams* (1962), 33
Czyżewska, Elżbieta: in *Gold Dreams* (1962), *34*, 37; in *The Saragossa Manuscript* (1965), 52

Davis, Bette, 109
Days of Wine and Roses (1962), 12
Dean, James, 12
Decalogue, The (1988), 84–85, 112
Deneuve, Catherine, 109

Dmochowski, Mariusz, in *The Doll* (1968), 65–66, 66
Doll, The (*Lalka*, 1968), 65–70, 107, 117, **124**; comparison with other films, 65, 70, 98; multiple formats of novel, 134n5; music and sound design, 70
Donkey Playing the Lyre (Pascal), 109, 111
Double Lives, Second Chances (Insdorf), 3
Douglas, Bill, 101
Drojecka, Wieslawa, in *One Room Tenants* (1960), 24
Dygat, Stanisław, 15, 21
Dylewska, Jolanta, 110
Dymna, Anna, in *Memoirs of a Sinner* (1986), 99

East European Film Bulletin, 107
Ebert, Roger, 12
Edelman, Paweł, 110
Eichlerówna, Irena, and *Codes* (1966), 57
Emerson, Ralph Waldo, 52
Era New Horizons, 5
existentialism, 3–4, 7, 8, 18, 24–25, 53, 70, 83, 88
Exorcist (1973), 53
Eyes Wide Shut (1999), 67

Fabulous Journey of Balthazar Kober, The (*Niezwykła podróz Baltazara Kobera*, 1988), 103–7, 109, **126**; comparison with other films, 104, 105–6, 107
Farewells (*Pożegnania*, 1958), 5–6, 15–19, 107, **121**; characteristics of films, 4–6, 10–11, 19, 35–36; comparison with other films, 15, 16, 17–19, 22–23, 30–31, 35–37; honors and awards, 4, 5, 19; music and sound design, 16, 18, 19
Fellini, Federico, 36, 74
Figgis, Mike, 12
Figura, Katarzyna, in *Memoirs of a Sinner* (1986), 99
Fijewski, Tadeusz, 129n2 (chap. 1); in *The Doll* (1968), 65; in *Gold Dreams* (1962), 33, 37; in *The Noose* (1957), 8, 10
Film Comment, 54, 106
film noir, 5, 28
Film Polski, 109
Film Quarterly, 77
Film Society of Lincoln Center (New York City), 3
Film Workshop of the Young (Kraków), 115

FIPRESCI Award, 18
First Harvest (*Pierwszy plon*, 1950), 117, **127**
First Irish Theatre Festival (New York), 81
Ford, John, 8, 111
French New Wave, 5
Friedkin, William, 53

Gajda, Mieczysław, in *One Room Tenants* (1960), 21, 22, 25
Gajos, Janusz, in *An Uneventful Story* (1983), 83
Gałczyński, Konstanty Ildefonse, 22
Garbicz, Adam, 77
Garcia, Jerry, 47, 132nn1–2
Generation, A (1955), 33
German Expressionism, 5
Gliński, Robert, 110–11
Głowacki, Janusz, 13
Goddard, Michael, 109
Gold Dreams (*Złoto*, 1962), 33–38, **122**; comparison with other films, 33, 35–36, 36–37, 61; music and sound design, 36
Gombrowicz, Witold, 45
Grateful Dead, 47
Great Gatsby, The (1974), 73
Gréco, Juliette, 19
Gross, Darren, 132
Grünberg, Sławomir, 113
Grzegorzek, Mariusz, 55, 111–12
Guardian, 54
Guérin-Castel, Anne, 102, 107
Gugala, Tomasz, 113

Haliński, Andrzej: and *The Hourglass Sanatorium* (1973), 77–78, 80, 111; and *An Uneventful Story* (1983), 84; and *Write and Fight* (1985), 89–90
Haltof, Marek, 5, 11–12, 24, 66
Hamlet (Shakespeare), 39–41, 43, 44
Harmony (*Harmonia*, 1948), 116, **127**
Hartowicz, Hanna Kosińska, 4, 111
Harvard Film Archive, 47
Has, Stanisław (father), 60, 80, 107
Has, Wanda (wife), 79–81, 107, 109
Has, Wojciech Jerzy: birth, 4; cameo in *Gold Dreams* (1962), 35; death, 109, 111–12; described, 4; filmography, **121–27**; honors and awards, 6, 87–88; and Jewish traditions, 79–82, 112; at Łódź Film School, 109–13, 115; period of creative inactivity, 88; relationship with father, 60, 80, 107; retrospectives,

3, 5, 13–14, 47; training, 115. *See also
names of specific films*
Hasidic Jews, 3, 71–72, 78, 78–80
Has-ufki, 111
Helman, Alicja, 87, 102
Hemingway, Ernest, 12
Herbalists from Stone Valley (*Zielarze z
Kamiennej Doliny*, 1952), 118–19, **127**
Hiroshima, mon amour (1959), 39, 131n1
(chap. 6)
Hłasko, Marek, 7, 12–13, 83
Hoberman, J., 47
Hodge, Nick, 82
Hogg, James, 97, 100, 101–2
Holocaust, 17, 45, 58–59, 60, 71, 79, 81
Holoubek, Gustaw: in *The Fabulous
Journey of Balthazar Kober* (1988),
103; in *Farewells* (1958), 15; in *The
Hourglass Sanatorium* (1973), 71, 75–
76; in *The Noose* (1957), 3, 7–11; in
One Room Tenants (1960), 21–22, 25;
in *Out of a Dream, a Dream* (1998),
29; in *Partings* (1961), 27; in *The
Saragossa Manuscript* (1965), 48, 55; in
An Uneventful Story (1983), 83, 85, 87;
in *Write and Fight* (1985), 89, 90
Hourglass Sanatorium, The (*Sanatorium
pod klepsydrą*, 1973), 3, 29, 56, 69,
71–82, **124–25**; comparison with other
films, 73, 74, 77, 78, 86, 89, 94, 100,
106, 107, 116; honors and awards, 82,
87–88, 111; music and sound design,
74
How to Be Loved (*Jak być kochaną*,
1963), 4, 5–6, 27, 33, 39–45, 65, **123**;
comparison with other films, 39, 41,
43–44, 74, 84, 132n5 (chap. 6); honors
and awards, 44, 129n8; music and
sound design, 41, 43, 131n3 (chap. 6)
Huston, John, 111

Ida (2013), 6, 133–134n2
Igar, Stanisław, in *The Saragossa
Manuscript* (1965), 52
I'll Cry Tomorrow (1955), 12
Indeks Foundation, 113
Inquisition, 48, 50–51, 53, 56, 103–5, 107
Iwaszkiewicz, Jarosław, 79

Jabłoński, Dariusz, 112
Jahoda, Mieczysław: and *Codes* (1966),
61; and *Farewells* (1958), 16–17; and
Herbalists from Stone Valley (1952),

119; and *Jan's Bird Feeder* (1952), 119;
and *The Noose* (1957), 3–4, 8, 119;
and *The Saragossa Manuscript* (1965),
47, 133n13
Jamrozik, Żaneta, 45, 131n1 (chap. 6)
Janczar, Tadeusz, 17; in *Farewells* (1958),
15, 16
Jankowski, Jan, in *Memoirs of a Sinner*
(1986), 97
Jan's Bird Feeder (*Karmik Jankovy*, 1952),
118, 119, **127**
January Uprising (1863–64), 66
Jaworski, Wojciech, 109

Kabbalists, 48, 55–56, 80, 107
Kafka, Franz, 111
Kalinowska, Izabela, 53–56, 133n12
Kanał (1958), 17
Kardzis, Robert, 5
Karwowski, Łukasz, 110
Kaszycki, Lucjan: and *Farewells* (1958),
19; and *Gold Dreams* (1962), 36; and
One Room Tenants (1960), 24; and
Partings (1961), 28, 131n3 (chap. 4)
Kaufman, Philip, 3
Kawalerowicz, Jerzy, 119
Kędzierski, Grzegorz, 6; and *The Fabulous
Journey of Balthazar Kober* (1988),
103; and *Memoirs of a Sinner* (1986),
98; and *An Uneventful Story* (1983),
84–85, 88, 135nn1–2 (chap. 11); and
Write and Fight (1985), 89–90, 94,
135n2 (chap. 12)
Keough, Peter, 51–52
Kern, Ludwik Jerzy, and *Partings* (1961),
28–29
Kieślowski, Krzysztof, 3–4, 5, 84–85, 112
Kijowski, Andrzej, and *Codes* (1966), 57
Kijowski, Janusz, 102, 110
Kilar, Wojciech, and *The Doll* (1968), 70
Kino, 24
Kino Skarpa (Warsaw), 111
Kinski, Klaus, 111
Kluba, Henryk, 109
Kobiela, Bogumił: in *Farewells* (1958),
17–18; in *The Saragossa Manuscript*
(1965), 52, 55–56
Komar, Michal, and *Memoirs of a Sinner*
(1986), 97
Konarski, Feliks, 43
Kondrat, Tadeusz: in *The Doll* (1968), 69;
in *The Hourglass Sanatorium* (1973),
69, 71

Kornatowska, Maria, 4, 24, 27, 113; and
    Out of a Dream, a Dream (1998), 29
Kowalski, Władysław: in *Gold Dreams*
    (1962), 33, 34, 37; in *Partings* (1961),
    27, 28, 131n1 (chap. 4)
Kownacka, Gabriela, in *Write and Fight*
    (1985), 92
Kozłowski, Maciej, in *Memoirs of a Sinner*
    (1986), 97
Krafftówna, Barbara: in *Codes* (1966),
    57; in *Gold Dreams* (1962), 33; in
    How to Be Loved (1963), 39, 40, 42,
    44–45, 131n4; in *Out of a Dream, a
    Dream* (1998), 29; in *The Saragossa
    Manuscript* (1965), 50
Kraków Film Institute, 115
Kraków Post, 82
Krakowski, Andrzej, 112
Krakowski, Janusz, 112
Krawcyzk, Jadwiga, in *The Saragossa
    Manuscript* (1965), 52
Krawczyńka, Danuta, in *Partings* (1961),
    30
Kreczmar, Jan: in *Codes* (1966), 57, 62; in
    The Doll (1968), 65
Kryński, Sławomir, 12, 80, 112
Kubrick, Stanley, 53, 65, 67
Kuczyński, Adam, and *Out of a Dream, a
    Dream* (1998), 29
Kultura, 12
Kusturica, Emir, 92–93
Kwiatkowski, Tadeusz, 47
Kyrou, Ado, 5

Lankosz, Borys, 110
Łapicki, Andrzej: in *The Doll* (1968), 65,
    117; in *First Harvest* (1950), 117
La religieuse (1971), 53
Last Metro, The (1980), 41
La Strada (1954), 36
"Last Sunday, The," 36
Leaving Las Vegas (1995), 12
Le feu follet (*The Fire Within*, 1963), 7
Lincoln, Abraham, 22
Litka, Piotr, 115
Locarno International Film Festival, 18
Locomotive (*Parowóz Pt 47*, 1949), 116,
    127
Łódź Film School, 4, 6, 12, 55, 80, 102,
    109–11, 119
London, Jack, 35
Lonsdale, Michael, in *The Fabulous
    Journey of Balthazar Kober* (1988), 103

Lopate, Phillip, 54
Lost Weekend, The (1945), 12
Łubieńska, Anna: in *Farewells* (1958),
    19; in *One Room Tenants* (1960),
    21–22

Macbeth (Shakespeare), 101
Machulski, Jan, in *The Doll* (1968), 67
Majewski, Lech, 107
Makarczyński, Tadeusz, 117
Maklakiewicz, Zdzisław: in *Gold Dreams*
    (1962), 34; in *One Room Tenants*
    (1960), 21
Maksymiuk, Jerzy, 86; and *The Hourglass
    Sanatorium* (1973), 74; and *Memoirs
    of a Sinner* (1986), 98; and *Write and
    Fight* (1985), 93
Malle, Louis, 7
Man in the Window, The (Uniłowski), 23
martial law (1981), 45, 109
Masina, Giulietta, 36
Matyjaszkiewicz, Stefan: and *The Doll*
    (1968), 66; and *Gold Dreams* (1962),
    36; and *Partings* (1961), 28
Mavor, James, 101
Mazierska, Ewa, 5, 25, 36, 109
Mellin, Andrzej, 110
Melville, David, 79, 101–2
Memoirs of a Sinner (*Osobisty pamiętnik
    grzesznika przez niego samego spisany*,
    1986), 97–102, 107, **126**; comparison
    with other films, 98, 100, 105–6
Michałek, Bolesław, 31
Michalowski, Janusz, in *Memoirs of a
    Sinner* (1986), 97
Mikuć, Hanna, in *An Uneventful Story*
    (1983), 84
Milewska, Anna, in *An Uneventful Story*
    (1983), 83
Milski, Stanisław, 17; in *The Noose*
    (1957), 8
Młodnicki, Artur, in *How to Be Loved*
    (1963), 41
Mobia, Steve, 75, 79
Munk, Andrzej, 112, 119
Muslims, 48, 50–53, 56
My City (*Moje miasto*, 1950), 117, **127**

Napoléon Bonaparte, 68
Napoleonic Wars, 47
Nazis and Nazism, 33, 39, 41–42, 57, 63,
    79, 115
Nerval, Gérard de, 44

Netto, Irena: in *Farewells* (1958), 17, 30;
     in *One Room Tenants* (1960), 21, 30;
     in *Partings* (1961), 29–30, *30*
New Wave, 5
New Yiddish Rep, 81
New York Film Festival, 3, 4, 47
Niemczyk, Leon, in *The Saragossa
     Manuscript* (1965), 48
Noose, The (*Pętla*, 1957), 3–4, 5, 6, 7–14,
     119, **121**; comparison with other
     films, 12, 15, 16, 19, 25–26, 33, 35–
     36, *36*, 37, 39, 55, 56, 63, 65, 83, 84,
     87, 88, 89, 100; honors and awards,
     13–14; music and sound design, 11;
     production design, 8–11
Nosferatu (1922), 111
Nowicki, Jan: in *The Hourglass
     Sanatorium* (1973), 71, 72; in *Out of a
     Dream, a Dream* (1998), 29
Nurczyńska-Fidelska, Ewelina, 11–12

O'Brien, John, 12
"Ode to Joy" (Beethoven), 49
O'Donaghue, Darragh, 53, 55–56
Oedipus, 100
One Room Tenants, or *Roommates*
     (*Wspólny pokój*, 1960), 21–26, 77,
     122; comparison with other films, 22–
     23, 25–26, 37, 61, 89, 100; music and
     sound design, 24, 28, 130nn3–4
"On the Bridge," 24
Orientalist idiom, 54, 133n12
Origin, 81
Orska, Irena: in *The Hourglass
     Sanatorium* (1973), 29; in *Out of a
     Dream, a Dream* (1998), 29
Ostrowska, Elżbieta, 67, 70, 134n4 (chap.
     9)
Our Class (Słobodzianek), 44
Out of a Dream, a Dream (1998), 29

Pacific Film Archive, 47
"Pamiętasz, była jesień" ("Remember, It
     Was Autumn"), 19, 24, 28, 130nn3–4
Partings (*Rozstanie*, 1961), 27–31, 77,
     122; comparison with other films, 30–
     31, 94–95; music and sound design,
     28–29; production design, 30–31
Pascal, Blaise, 109
Pawlikowski, Adam, 17–18; in *Farewells*
     (1958), 30–31; in *Gold Dreams* (1962),
     35; in *One Room Tenants* (1960), 21,
     22, 25; in *Partings* (1961), 30; in *The*

Saragossa Manuscript (1965), 48, 49,
     55–56, 107
Pawlikowski, Paweł, 6, 133n2
Peña, Richard, 3
Penderecki, Krzysztof, 53, 62
Peszek, Jan, in *Write and Fight* (1985), 89
Photographer (1998), 112
Pieczka, Franciszek: in *Memoirs of a
     Sinner* (1986), 97, 99; in *The Saragossa
     Manuscript* (1965), 48
Pieracki, Józef, 18
Pietruski, Ryszard, in *One Room Tenants*
     (1960), 21
Plocki, Andrzej, and *The Hourglass
     Sanatorium* (1973), 77
Pluciński, Ryszard: and *Farewells* (1958),
     19, 24; and *One Room Tenants* (1960),
     24
Polanski, Roman, 3, 6, 12
Polish National Cinema (Haltof), 11–12
Polish school, 119, 136n3 (app.)
Poręba, Bohdan, 80
Potocki, Jan, 47, 54, 56
Potoroczyn, Pawel, 3
*Private Memoirs and Confessions of a
     Justified Sinner, The* (Hogg), 97
Prus, Boleslaw, 65, 66, 68
Przegrodzki, Igor, in *The Noose* (1957), 8
Przybylska, Sława, 19; and *Partings*
     (1961), 28
Putowski, Maciej, 112; and *Codes* (1966),
     60; and *The Doll* (1968), 67; and *The
     Hourglass Sanatorium* (1973), 78, 80

Rankin, Ian, 101
Rationalism, 54
"Red Clouds" ("Czerwone chmury"), 24, 28
Red Desert (1964), 36
Red Shields (Iwaszkiewicz), 79
"Remember, It Was Autumn," 19, 24, 28
Restivo, Justin, 132n5 (chap. 6)
Riva, Emmanuelle, in *The Fabulous
     Journey of Balthazar Kober* (1988), 104
Rivette, Jacques, 53
Robinson, Isabel, 7–8, 10–11, 52–53, 75
Roddick, Nick, 13–14
Romańczuk, Elwira, in *An Uneventful
     Story* (1983), 83
Roommates. See *One Room Tenants,* or
     Roommates (*Wspólny pokój*, 1960)
Rota, Nino, 36
Różewicz, Stanisław, 115
Rushdie, Salman, 54

Samson (1961), 41, 45
Sanatorium under the Sign of the Hourglass (Schulz), 71
San Francisco International Film Festival, 44, 129n8, 132n2
Saragossa Manuscript, The (*Rękopis znaleziony w Saragossie*, 1965), 3, 6, 47–56, 77, **123**; comparison with other films, 55–56, 73, 77, 78, 100, 104, 107; honors and awards, 47, 132nn1–2; music and sound design, 49, 53; production design, 50
Sartre, Jean-Paul, 25
Schrader, Paul, 106
Schulz, Bruno, 71, 74–77, 79, 80, 82, 134n3 (chap. 10)
Scorsese, Martin, 6, 47, 53
"Second Coming, The" (Yeats), 56
Seniuk, Anna, in *The Doll* (1968), 67–68
Shakespeare, William, 39–41, 43, 44, 101
Shinint, The (1980), 53
Shutter Island (2010), 53
Sight and Sound, 14
Simón del Desierto (1965), 47
Sjöström, Victor, 61
Skarżanka, Hanna, in *Farewells* (1958), 17
Skarżński, Jerzy: and *The Hourglass Sanatorium* (1973), 77; and *Partings* (1961), 30
Skarżyńska, Lidia, and *The Hourglass Sanatorium* (1973), 77
Skolimowski, Jerzy, 36
Skorupski, Grzegorz, 4
Śląska, Aleksandra, 8
Słobodzianek, Tadeusz, 44
Sobociński, Piotr, and *An Uneventful Story* (1983), 84–85
Sobociński, Witold: and *Codes* (1966), 61; and *The Hourglass Sanatorium* (1973), 71, 77
Sokołowska, Helena, in *Farewells* (1958), 17
Stankówna, Hanna, in *Memoirs of a Sinner* (1986), 97
Starkówna, Irena, in *Farewells* (1958), 15
Steam Engine (*Parowóz Pt 47*, 1949), 116, **127**
surrealism, 3, 5–6, 49–50, 53–55, 67, 71, 73
Swan Lake (Tchaikovsky), 41, 43
Szmigielówna, Teresa, in *The Noose* (1957), 8

Szpak, Wlodzimierz, 110
Szumowska, Malgorzata, 110, 111

Tchaikovsky, Pyotr Iyich, 41, 43
Tchórzewski, Krzystof, 110
Tencer, Gołda, 81
Terlecki, Władisław, and *Write and Fight* (1985), 89, 92
Thompson, Nathaniel, 132
Three Colors: Blue, White, Red (1993), 5, 84–85
Three Sisters (Chekhov), 65
Time of the Gypsies (1988), 92–93
Toeplitz, Krzysztof Teodor, 37
Traces (2012), 5, 107, 110
Tristan, Frédérick, 103, 104
Truffaut, François, 3
Trybala, Marzena, in *Write and Fight* (1985), 92
Trzaskalski, Piotr, 110
Turaj, Frank, 31
Tyszkiewicz, Beata: in *The Doll* (1968), 65, 66; in *One Room Tenants* (1960), 21; in *The Saragossa Manuscript* (1965), 50

"Umarli są wśród nas" ("The Dead Are Among Us," Hłasko), 13
Uneventful Story, An (*Nieciekawa historia*, 1983), 83–88, 119, **125**; comparison with other films, 65, 83, 84, 86, 87, 88, 89; music and sound design, 70, 86
Uniłowski, Zbigniew, 21, 23
Updike, John, 76
Ustinov, Peter, 109

Village Voice, 47
voyeurism, 68, 78, 93, 98

Wachowiak, Maria, in *Farewells* (1958), 15, *16*, 19
Waiting for Godot (Beckett), 81
Wajda, Andrzej, 3; and *Ashes and Diamonds* (1958), 11, 17–19, 36–37, 43–44, 55–56; and *A Generation*, 33; and *Samson* (1961), 45
Wakeman, John, 115
Walkover (1965), 36
Walt Disney films, 115
Wardejn, Zdzisław, in *Write and Fight* (1985), 89
Warsaw Ghetto, 45, 58, 110

Warsaw Uprising, 17
Welles, Orson, 109
Wieczyński, Rafal, in *The Fabulous Journey of Balthazar Kober* (1988), 103, *105*, 136n1 (chap. 14)
Wieniewska, Celina, 76
Wilder, Billy, 12
Wild Strawberries (1957), 61
Wiśniewska, Ewa, in *Memoirs of a Sinner* (1986), 99
Wójcik, Jerzy, 119
Wołyniec, Roman, and *The Noose* (1957), 8–9
World War I, 55, 60, 69, 89, 90
World War II, 15, 39, 43, 45, 53, 55, 57–58, 60–61, 71, 77, 79, 81
Write and Fight (*Pismak*, 1985), 89–95, **125**; comparison with other films, 89, 94–95, 100; music and sound design, 92–93
Wysocka, Lidia, in *Partings* (1961), 27, *28*, *30*
Wysocki, Wojciech, in *Write and Fight* (1985), 89, *90*, *91*

Yeats, W. B., 56
Yiddish, 21–22, 78–81

Zamachowski, Zbigniew, in *The Fabulous Journey of Balthazar Kober* (1988), 104, *105*
Zanussi, Krzysztof, 3, 4
Zelnik, Jan, 117
Zelnik, Jerzy, in *Write and Fight* (1985), 92
Żylinska, Jadwiga, 27